CW00549600

1 MONTH OF
FREE
READING

at

www.ForgottenBooks.com

By purchasing this book you are eligible for one month membership to ForgottenBooks.com, giving you unlimited access to our entire collection of over 1,000,000 titles via our web site and mobile apps.

To claim your free month visit: www.forgottenbooks.com/free136571

ISBN 978-1-5284-8223-3
PIBN 10136571

LIFE'S QUESTIONINGS

A BOOK OF EXPERIENCE

BY

WILLIAM ROMAINE PATERSON

(BENJAMIN SWIFT)

METHUEN & CO.

36 ESSEX STREET W.C.

LONDON

First Published in 1905

NOTE

IN offering this book to those to whom Life may
have made a similar appeal, the Author ventures to repeat these words: *J'écrirai ici mes
pensées sans ordre, et non pas peut-être dans une
confusion sans dessein; c'est le véritable ordre, et
qui marquera toujours mon objet par le désordre
même.*

LIFE'S QUESTIONINGS

AS far as possible we should conduct our minds on Free Trade principles, and lay no tariff even on hostile opinion. Nevertheless, the soul turns wearily on the sickbed of theories.

No doubt it is well to warn the soul that it shall live better by renunciation. But perpetual subtraction means zero at last. And if we empty the soul of all its desires, we convert it into a shadow and a simulacrum, a shrivelled and abstract thing hardly related to human conditions. We may keep washing the soul white until it is in rags.

It is startling to think of the heavy, rough, actual wood of the Cross, and to observe that now the Cross has become only a symbol, and is decked with silken tassels and little velvet flags, and is guaranteed easy for carrying. Moreover,

A   I

its victory was assured when it was accepted among the world's trinkets and worn as jewellery.

Immortality might be the soul's *second wind*.

The soul is hardly like the vine, which accepts even the poorest soil which common weeds disdain. The vine will grow among stones, because the stones which have stored up heat in the daytime give it back at night, and the vine is kept warm until dawn. But the conditions are harder for the soul in this night of life. It cannot always reject or transform the poisoned soil into which its roots have been plunged. Evil, in order to be rejected, must first be admitted into the soul. Herein lies the immense menace to an organism whose process of absorption is Reflection. Once the larvæ of lies have been deposited, how they multiply!

It is a strange fact that those who work with poisonous substances are more liable to become insane. If, therefore, the soul is in contact with all the irritants of life, drugged with its passion and the *nux vomica* of its hatreds, we should scarcely wonder at its toxic condition.

2

Unbelief may be a kind of bad manners of the soul, and those who disbelieve in God are rude.

Cynicism is of no great importance. There is truth in cynicism, but it is cramped and distorted. We must reach the cynicism of cynicism.

Nothing breeds so quickly as ice.

Plato shows that intense pleasure deprives a man of the use of his faculties.

Dogmatism appears to produce in the dog-matist a kind of intellectual lockjaw.

Truth often requires imposture to help it on.

If a knave behaves politely to us there is a danger of thinking him less a knave.

Passion is the boa-constrictor of the soul, and brings about the strangulation of the will.

3

Leopardi points out that the use of the phrase "the world" to denote the enemy of all that is noble in the soul first appears in the Gospels. No Greek or Paynim philosopher arrived at the same conception. Epictetus, however, surely touches it.

In discussing pleasure and pain, Socrates shows that he who pursues either is compelled to accept both.

Good drama does not consist in dividing the sheep from the goats by an impassable barrier. The human drama exists because there is a perpetual oscillation of good and evil in the same being.

The Ideal is never *here*, but *there*. It is not an inn at which we can put up. It is a journey.

There is some consolation in the belief that if a prize were offered for the most evil deed imaginable, the majority of men, even although guaranteed against punishment, would shrink from being competitors.

4

Society is full of opposing forces which destroy or paralyse each other like sea currents.

We must accept the fact that in all life there is pre-established discord as well as pre-established harmony.

Sometimes when the soul has acquired a new truth it hastens to strut with it as with a peacock's feather.

A terrible spiritual ossification threatens us after long contact with the world. Owing to the repetition of impressions we become numb and irresponsive.

At the banquet of life so many of the meats are poisoned that the soul, becoming afraid, feigns not to be hungry.

Qui a terre a guerre.

When I hear certain men talking about "principles," I wonder whether they do not mean "prejudices" elevated to that high rank.

5

Supposing we reach a philosophic view of things, should the shape of the minds and of the characters of human beings irritate us any more than the deformities of their bodies? In the one case as in the other uncontrollable causes may have been at work.

Passion promises worlds, and gives nothing, and its gold is fairy gold.

The soul has two windows, one that looks towards the radiant and the other towards the infernal regions. The philosopher has the courage to pull up the blinds of both those windows.

Hope, like a homing bird, comes punctually back even with torn plumage.

I observe thousands of my fellow-men running to help the *strong*.

La Rochefoucauld often withers the truth in the glacial atmosphere of cynicism; Chamfort sometimes imperils it in the blaze of his epigram; La Bruyère, more sober and less brilliant than

6

either of them, saves it by moderation. But Chamfort, because of the high human temperature of his writing, is the greatest of the three.

The world is rough, and Ideals become foot-sore.

Men like Byron, Nietzsche, Chamfort, and Giordano Bruno appear to have had a perpetual thunderstorm in their minds.

It has been calculated that about 150,000 people die every day.

Let not those who traffic with the food of the poor forget that for every fall of two shillings per bushel in the price of wheat the death-rate falls three per cent.

The meaning of the History of Thucydides is this : Athens did not know how to be wise in prosperity, and therefore she fell.

The soul, like an athlete, must always be *training*.

There are some things we cannot disguise without ruining them. We cannot disguise honey in gall. This is the answer to Jesuitism.

Aber, ist denn die Welt ein Guck-Kasten?

The stars do not need the astronomer, but the astronomer needs the stars.

Aristotle gave a piquant definition of wit, which he called " cultured insolence."

The existence of smuggling is a sign that custom dues are found to be excessive. When Rockingham reduced them in the American colonies smuggling almost ceased. This is a proof that, on the whole, human beings are reasonable.

Two clocks may chime the same hour, and both may be wrong. In order to fortify ourselves in some bad opinion we often deliberately seek the agreement of those who are as ill-instructed as ourselves.

Even the bright sky has its burden of dead stars.

Tragedy turns the Fairies into Furies, and Comedy turns the Furies into Fairies.

The theatre should be the least theatrical of all the arts because it is able to reduce to a minimum the difference between reality and illusion. Emotions are not merely portrayed, but they are identified with actual human beings and embodied in them. Instead of listening to narratives or looking at pictures, we actually see persons and events.

Aristotle has a beautiful definition of Comedy. He says it is the business of Comedy to make friends of those who were enemies. I do not know whether he said that it is the business of Tragedy to make enemies of those who might have been friends, but that also seems to be true. At any rate, the drama sums up our existence as no other art does, because Comedy and Tragedy are the most vivid expression of all that social conditions imply. They are the dramatic exhibition of human pleasure and of human pain. It is therefore obvious that Tragedy can never be really popular. At least a modern audience

9

is not prepared to discover in it that educative purpose which seems to have impressed two such different men as Aristotle and Napoleon. It is an interesting fact that Napoleon found intense pleasure in Tragedy. He said he would have made Corneille a prince. But his interest in the tragic stage was doubtless morbid, whereas Aristotle believed that its real value consists in its warning against the catastrophes of passion. The modern world, however, has become more sensitive to physical and to spiritual torture. There are even those who raise the question: "Should Tragedy be exhibited at all?" Now it cannot be maintained that Tragedy should not be exhibited because it is untrue. It would be ridiculous to say that in the world there exists nothing but the material for Comedy—unless, indeed, Comedy means what Balzac made it mean. In that case it includes not merely "revel" but "tragic revel." It is easy for epic writers like Goethe, for instance, to warn us that we should "see life whole." A whole is made up of two parts, and it is our misfortune that the two parts often fall asunder and refuse to coalesce. It is for that reason that some dramatists express themselves first in a series of comedies and then in a series of tragedies. It was the opinion of Socrates that the great dramatist must write both. Think of the extraordinary difference of mood which separates *The Merry Wives of Windsor* from *Timon of Athens*. The mind which created both has, in the interval which divides them, gone over many a jolting road. But the reasons which, in certain cases, might justifiably preclude the exhibition of Tragedy are not philosophic but æsthetic. Men shrink from spectacular contortion. The preference for Comedy is the result of the instinct of self-preservation and of the determination of society to eliminate disaster from its midst. What can it do, for instance, with the gallery of horrors which some of the Elizabethans built ? In Ford and Webster and Tourneur a whole menagerie of crimes is let loose upon the stage. The sumptuous language of the Elizabethans seems only to increase the terror. It is as if we were to deck an infernal machine with roses. Yet Webster and Ford are great names, although perhaps Hazlitt and Lamb were too exorbitant in their eulogy of them. Webster and Ford were men who, after having looked intensely at human life, came to the conclusion that the material for Tragedy accumulates at a greater rate and in greater volume than the material for Comedy. It is indisputable. But there is no reason in *art*, although there is great reason in science, why we should be asked to take sudden and terrible plunges into human character.

In science, indeed, we must know everything, and hide nothing. It is perhaps wise to admit frankly, however, that art is not so much truth as a selection of it, and a selection which implies an omission. Art is really a mirage. It is an attempt to shelter Beauty from Ugliness. In books—in the psychological novel, for example—the analysis must be allowed to go full length. Science and art are in such a case working together. But in the theatre the visual shock must be mitigated for the sake of human comfort. Ford and Webster keep the black flag flying for ever. We read them when we are in danger of forgetting that this may be the worst of all possible worlds. Who will deny, however, that Comedy is the necessary antiseptic? He who has the chance of laughter, and misses it, is apparently a fool. The greatest modern writer of Comedy is Molière. Now, we know from contemporary evidence—from Boileau, for instance, and from Chapelle and from Mademoiselle Poisson—that Molière was profoundly melancholy. His domestic life was terribly embittered. He was no doubt very successful, but he was also disenchanted. Moreover, although he never could have been a great tragic actor, he might have been a great tragic writer, as we see from *Le Festin de Pierre*. Yet, in spite of all this, Molière decided that the theatre should not be

made the scene of horror and distress. There is
hardly a trace of melancholy in his works, except
perhaps in the most autobiographic of these,
George Dandin. But even *George Dandin* is
full of laughter. In short, after we have read
Molière, we begin to believe that the ónly death
to deplore is the death of humour.

Nemesis is punctual. She is the only woman
who keeps her appointments.

There are some persons who refuse to become
meek until they are convinced that the Meek do
really inherit the earth.

It is in vain we cry "Woa! woa!" to the wild
horses of Illusion.

There are occasions when a man's defects, not
his qualities, make his fortune.

.Equality and Liberty are not the same thing,
and may be actually antagonistic. If in a community there happen to be certain men more
highly endowed than others, then, to restrict the

natural use of these endowments is to deny them liberty. But to permit the use of them will create inequalities of social condition, because some men will rise where others will fall. Equality, therefore, is the enemy of Liberty, and Liberty makes Equality impossible. And yet in the *Contrat Social* Rousseau makes the ridiculous statement: "La Liberté ne peut subsister sans l'égalité."

In the structure of Society some men seem to fill important places, but they are like caryatides in architecture, and only *appear* to hold up the building.

Life is very short, but the hours are very long.

The starry sky is only a façade. There are stars behind stars.

By dwelling in cities men cease to become familiar with Immensity.

After *thirty*, the wells of illusion are not so full.

14

Some of the problems of life may be solved by good manners.

Love holds the map to half the *terra damnata* of the human soul.

Love is a reckless tenant of the soul, and leaves a huge dilapidation bill.

All lovers meet in the magnetic meridian.

Cheap wines intoxicate soonest.

The history of mankind is mainly the history of Property. The human race has constituted itself the collective guardian of chattels, and this is the cause of war.

Napoleon's campaigns involved the deaths of two million soldiers.

We would all rather lose our temper than our purse.

It is a strange paradox that sometimes we are too tired even to sleep.

Often little children are specially terror-stricken at the apparition of very old persons. There is some deep meaning in this.

There appear to be cases where conscience goes to pieces with mere old age like any other bit of furniture.

Conscience seems to play in the moral life the part which memory plays in the mind.

The soul scarcely knows all it contains of darkness and strong mystery.

If there were no death would there be so many religions?

Apprentices to pastry cooks are at first permitted to eat as many sweets as they please, because after a short time they begin to have an aversion for all such things. What a comment on the duration of pleasure!

Metchnikoff has an audacious and terrible definition of Man. He says that "Man is a kind of miscarriage of an ape."

Ideals are the things which breed least, and are in most danger of becoming extinct.

The best way to destroy some passions is to gratify them.

One advantage of being obscure is that we are *incognito* all the year round.

There is something unnatural in a woman who refuses to gossip.

Love is a disease, marriage the remedy, and sometimes the remedy is worse than the disease.

Some virtues are like suits of armour which are handed down from father to son.

Death is all the world's rendezvous.

Perhaps the artist should be like the sundial, *horas non numerat nisi serenas.*

Molière sows ridicule with both hands.

It is an unfortunate circumstance that a bait involves a hook.

Almost all historical phenomena are morally piebald.

Philosophers tax their minds to discover unity in the scheme of things. But there is unity even in a thunderstorm, whose function is dissolution.

The Living forget that there are acres of dead and buried things throughout the world.

Liberty is always in danger.

The objection to a loan is that it must be repaid.

Blake's line, "The lost traveller's dream under the hill," is perhaps the most haunting in English poetry.

Grattan had a great phrase; he said, "There are some effulgent ideas."

Great art is never filthy. The pæan of existence is not to be sung by rotten lungs.

Life is so amazing that not one of the millions of human beings alive to-day has the same feeling about it. It affects them all differently. Nay, almost day after day each individual finds his own judgment about it changing.

The soul is still searching for moorings in the open sea.

There are herald devils as well as herald angels.

A man's jealousy is what a woman often finds easy to forgive, and sometimes she hardly forgives him unless he is jealous.

Quarrelling appears to be one of the chief occupations of lovers.

19

Fashion is always committing suicide, but, like the phœnix, it rises from its own ashes with every feather intact.

There is only one monster from which we must run away, and it is Dishonour.

Even the most powerful brain is only a candle illuminating a skull.

Everything is precarious.

A crown of roses is only the top of a crown of thorns.

It is foolish to say that Reason shall necessarily make us happy. It makes us often as unhappy as Passion.

Theologians hope that we all go at least zigzag to God, and even in their own case that sometimes happens.

Religion is an appeal *ad misericordiam* and *in forma pauperis*.

Can disease ever be really destroyed? Physicists know that a force once in being is always in being although it may change its form. Disease is one of the disintegrating forces of the universe. No doubt the phagocytes fight and destroy microbes, but the poison absorbed must be only temporarily neutralised, and awaits re-combination and a fresh diffusion. If this be true of moral poisons, creation must have the appearance of an eternal catastrophe.

Some of us share Hazlitt's detestation of those who cannot arrive at the comprehension of an abstract idea.

Wherever we go we discover an avenging principle either in the form of life or of death.

If Life is a gift, why should not Death be?

It is more than once that a man hears his own muffled drum in the distance.

The judgments of childhood are contradicted by those of youth, which, in turn, are corrected by those of manhood and old age. Which are true?

If we are conscious of indifference we are not wholly indifferent.

The serpent of suicide is never done wriggling through the ranks of men.

One milligramme of musk gives forth perfume for seven thousand years. One milligramme of radium gives forth light for seventy thousand years. And shall not the soul persevere?

The human tombstone has often the form of a point of exclamation.

We see a flower growing in the sunlight, and we forget the patient root toiling below.

That author is fortunate who is able to dedicate his ink-bottle to Comedy, for Blessed be Laughter.

There is something vulgar in selfishness.

Self-love is more exhausting than love for others.

The poor look with terror on the oncoming winter.

The poor have also *their* glorious youth, which they are compelled to pass in rags. They, too, have the sense of zenith and the sense of beauty outraged in misfortune.

The fatigue caused by hope prolonged is like the fatigue of standing on tiptoe for ever.

The duration of love as a passion does not seem to lie within our own control.

It is not true that the Pole star is fixed. It swings like a pendulum.

The human mind is able to face a clear issue, even though it be a hostile one. What wrecks and bewilders it is delay or ambiguity.

Conscience is a kind of vigilance committee of the mind.

23

Voltaire's intellect is the assassin among intellects.

When we meet two bores we should make sure that they shall entertain each other.

In more than one sphere of life, merry-go-round appears to be a euphemism for sorry-go-round.

It is only when it is in danger that you realise that your reputation is your greatest asset.

The human mind if thoroughly awake finds itself besieged by paradox.

In every life there is a steady advance towards some form of disillusion.

So-called certainties have a habit of becoming only probabilities, which in turn become improbabilities, and these degenerate first into bare possibilities and then into impossibilities until the fiasco is complete.

Compassion is the master feeling of all great souls.

Throughout all this fanfare of life we hear the *adagio lamentoso.*

There is an extraordinary line in Massinger: "I have put off from the shore of innocence."

It is a strange calamity for the soul when it has become too conscious of its centrifugal force, and gyrates at an immense distance from the Central Sun.

Of all things Thought appears to have the least market-value, and is allowed a place only in the sale of Remnants at the close of the day.

Certain men seem to have female characteristics, and to desire jewellery in the form of Decorations.

All around us there is an immense hubbub about insignificant things.

Those who judge Voltaire without having read his vast correspondence do not know him, and their opinion is worthless. To his age he was an intellectual necessity.

It is really remarkable that the coats of arms of civilised nations and of individuals should contain the portraits of savage beasts.

The most ironical fact in history is that gunpowder was the discovery of a monk.

Virtue is like a uniform which gives distinction even to the commonest.

Long after Faith has been lost the echoes of its departing footsteps linger in the soul, and they should be allowed to linger.

In its essence the universe appears to be explosive. Great catastrophes like earthquake and volcanic eruption have their counterpart, less theatrical but no less tragic, in the annihilations which take place every day in the world of organised beings.

The human organism, like every other organism, lives by plunder, and ultimately all enterprise is directed against the possibility of famine.

Every idealistic system rests upon an unexplored basis of realism. The philosophic idealist leaves behind far too much that is unexpiated. He hides the catastrophes, material and moral, which perpetually dislocate the scheme of things.

It is on a basis of injustice and aggression that the edifice of Justice has been raised. Property was accumulated long before the foundations of Law were even rudely laid, and long before a theory of Justice was evolved or practised.

He has a vast task of casuistry before him who attempts to discover the moral purpose of the slaughter-house.

We attempt to explain the world by means of the human mind. But this is only to attempt to explain one enigma by another.

The unknown is within us as well as outside of us.

Ultimately there is no reasoning except reasoning in a circle, because things are explained by each other and by their mutual presuppositions. Knowledge or science is like a dictionary in which we search the meaning of a word, and are sent to another for it, and then to another, until we come back to the word from which we started.

Where is the Centre of Immensity?

In the human mind we inherit a wonderful instrument, but it may have been damaged in the transmission.

The ego is the worm that dieth not.

Pessimism when organised into a system becomes a kind of metaphysical *Schadenfreude*. The Pessimist begins, like Schopenhauer, to find actual joy in any new discovery which appears to demonstrate the universality and the symmetry of evil.

The last ambush is Death.

28

No doubt our minds should be hospitable to new truth. Yet there are some doctrines against which the mind should establish a quarantine to prevent the spread of diseased opinion.

We should not be afraid to lay bare the contradictions in the soul, because the deepest minds have touched Scepticism as well as Belief, and they have traversed that " ocean of darkness " of which George Fox speaks.

Who doubts that conscience is the necessary spiritual disinfectant?

The sexual instinct has apparently no reference to the welfare of the individual.

It is a remarkable and saddening truth that contact with a higher civilisation is fatal to peoples in primitive conditions.

There is a profound saying of Feuerbach that " Love idealises matter and materialises spirit."

Perhaps it is because the secret of the universe is too astounding that it flees before the inquiry of the human soul.

Half our troubles are the result of our pretensions.

Certain men wish to live by their idealism, and the world makes them die of it.

Touch is the dumb alphabet of Love.

It is the privilege of the great to make their dependents intensely happy by insignificant gifts.

In youth the hours seem to have the room of centuries.

There are things which migrate like birds from the soul—youth, hope, love. Some come back, but youth is that bird of bright plumage which never returns.

There is a deadening monotony in the Tales of Love.

The love of scandal resembles the strange and abominable pleasure of scratching an itch.

Marriage is often a state of mutual surveillance.

To marry is to lead a double life.

There are certain marriages which should have been celebrated on Fool's Day.

The only human being whose love for you is disinterested and permanent is your mother.

Destiny is our sole destination.

Most written history seems to be as misleading as to-day's newspaper and as dead as yesterday's.

In reading Marat we seem to see his brain gnawing like a rodent at terrible things.

When Louis xiv. was exhumed he was "a black, indistinguishable mass of aromatics." O human greatness!

It is a sign of the fundamental wickedness of the human race that during the French Revolution small gold and silver guillotines were worn as jewellery by the women.

There are persons who suppose that they are mountaineering when they are walking on mole hills.

Some extremely respectable persons are all ballast and no cargo.

That was a wise provision in the Roman Army according to which the arms carried during peace were double the weight of those carried in war.

Spinoza seems to have been doubtful about the ethical value of repentance. And indeed it is often nearer to cowardice than to courage.

The abandonment of Polytheism may have had an economical origin. It was not merely the most expansive but the most expensive of all religions, since the multiplication of gods meant the multiplication of altars and of sacrifices.

The fact that the history of the world is such an immense volume is a proof that the world has been in great disorder.

Only a man like Cæsar could make love to a woman and carry on a war at the same time.

What an admission that is of Alexander Severus, the Roman Emperor: "Omnia fui, et nihil expedit"—"I was everything, and it profits me nothing."

Beneath the accumulation of "rights" lie murder, rapine, and the will of the stronger.

Some persons go to work with the thick end of the wedge.

The world is more interested in your personalty than in your personality.

Who supposes that the Future can ever arrive? The Future recedes.

It is possible to admire Chateaubriand's temperament but to feel doubtful about his character. The two things are quite different.

There is a strange pleasure in moderation, and it is not possible to sympathise with Kant's objection to the Greek doctrine of the Mean.

A man should ride the horse that has thrown him.

The human eye is often an uncharitable microscope. Nevertheless, there are some human beings who should be labelled "Poison."

It was not merely cynicism but the desire for historical accuracy which compelled Gibbon to point out that although the early Christians turned with horror from the sight of pagan

34

images, yet many of them accepted the Roman money, the reverse side of which was of an idolatrous nature.

Some of us commit suicide by living on.

It is extraordinary that after having lost belief in God men are able to believe in themselves.

For all we know, our words may be dim symbols for enormous realities.

That is a wonderful saying of Plato: "The soul is like a drunkard when she touches change."

History is a vast Almanac of Death.

Voltaire's *mot* on France is inimitable. He said France is "La crème fouettée de l'Europe."

Our minds and our bodies are perpetually suffering change, and all that seems to preserve our identity is the sense of vanity.

Autumn flowers have a sinister perfume like frozen opium.

To make it happy, the soul needs great doses of oblivion.

Je ne regarde la vie que comme un songe.

There are a few wise minds in which Scepticism and Belief are allowed to be the best of friends. The greatest of those minds was Eckhart's.

Let us never forget the greatness of Wycliffe. The soul, like a lollard, must go on singing its defiant psalm in the face of all obese and stagnant orthodoxies.

There is a kind of orthodoxy which insults God by pretending to understand Him.

That was a pardonable witticism of Schopenhauer when he spoke of "Die Ortodoxen Ochsen von Oxford."

The orthodox person puts his intelligence in handcuffs.

The world is so complex that no single judgment about it is true.

Human existence is often so solemn and suffering is so real that we are startled to discover that there does really exist an immense amount of the genuine material for laughter.

The History of Cruelty makes the soul aghast. Every day there is an immolation of living and quivering things.

It is difficult to trace a moral process in History. But since History is undoubtedly a chain of causes and effects, the logical or the illogical process is not difficult to discover.

All written History is an epitaph and a vast *Post Mortem.*

Many writers serve up a *Vin ordinaire* as if it were a great wine.

Michelet holds the Middle Age in the hollow of his hand. Many of the romantic writers hold it in the hollow of their brains.

On every summit there is peace, but especially on the summit of ignorance.

Good style is as firm as a diamond and deserves as much polishing.

A writer should be judged by his use of the adjective. The great writers have invariably concentrated upon the adjective, and they have a horror of over elaboration. Bad writers heap up the adjectives, whereas the great writers use only a few of them like sumpter mules, but load them with meaning.

There is a great phrase of Molière: "La vérité fait cabrer."

Human life may be dust, but it is magnetic dust.

Sculpture is a pathetic attempt to stem the sea of oblivion which washes over everything at last.

When we consider the immensity of the universe and the throng of stars, it is amazing that we should become so absorbed in trivialities.

The Dead lie like hermits in their cells.

It is a strange and beautiful fact that sick persons often find relief towards dawn, as if they are delivered from the oppression and sorcery of the night.

It is astonishing to think how much the façade costs us.

All meals appear to end in dessert or in some form of sugar. It is like the demand for the happy ending of a novel or of a play.

Buying and selling, no matter how honourably done, appear to leave a certain taint in human character. There is always a secret desire for advantage, and when the bargain is completed there is a smirk.

Stendhal points out that the mouths of money lovers are *d'une atroce laideur*.

There is a strange pleasure in looking at an honest face.

39

Conscience is a kind of sounding board set up in men's brains for moral acoustics, and guaranteed to make the weakest whisper heard all over the building.

Some of the letters we receive, and perhaps some of those we write, should conclude, " Yours unfaithfully," " Yours insincerely."

Some of the beliefs we have perhaps lost were so great that they should be at least embalmed.

It is useless to attempt to make special terms with Destiny.

Often by keeping time with other people we only lose it.

The world is always formidable.

Pascal has a beautiful definition of rivers. He says they are roads that march, *des chemins qui marchent.*

40

The beast of prey so terrible against other animals is full of tenderness for its young.

Of all literary characters André Chénier and Diderot appear to be the most lovable.

If thinkers were really courageous they would admit that they always reach a point where their theories become muddled.

Blake puts a pertinent question to the tiger: "Did He who made the lamb make thee?"

An atom is the Infinite without elbow room.

Children should be taught that to speak the truth is a sign of good breeding. The difficulty, however, is that that statement appears to be untrue to those who already know the world. Good manners are sometimes a hotbed of lies.

It is strange that although we all abhor a crush, there is a look of desperation on the face of a hostess whose Reception is only thinly attended.

The banquet of life is one of those dinner-parties which are overcrowded.

There do appear to be some cases in which it is necessary to be as wise as a serpent and as harmful.

There are certain persons who, like lepers, should be provided with a hand-bell to warn us of their approach.

In his *Second Defence of the English People*, Milton gives a most striking warning to Cromwell: " You shall never be able to be really free unless *we* are."

Molière is the most original of all plagiarists.

It is curious that the ancient Mexicans worshipped the cross long before they heard of Christianity. It was the symbol of their god of Rain.

The rejected lover is always dangerous.

Let the over-fed keep Lent. The poor are compelled to keep it continually.

No concert can be begun without the discord and hoarse tuning of the instruments.

We exhaust the Future by ardently desiring it. The pleasure it brings is already half consumed by the imagination.

Marriage is a sea in which there is a good deal of mixed bathing.

Fate is that fortune-teller whose lips are sealed until the events are passed.

If the Dead rise, it shall be with a shriek to find themselves back in an unhappy world.

Boileau offers excellent advice: " Jamais au spectateur n'offrez rien d'incroyable."

43

The universal life passes away like a torrent, and like a torrent remains.

There are parts of the earth, such as rocks, deserts, and cliffs, where Nature seems to have perished and to have left only a skeleton of herself.

Geologists calculate that it has taken the earth one hundred million years to arrive at its present condition.

The universe is leaking. There is a perpetual trickle of water through the floor of the sea.

The universe seems to be a vast system of nerves. During the earthquake at Lisbon the Swiss lakes and the lakes in America and in Finland, and all the seas and lakes of the world, heaved for hours in sympathy.

When the harness of Life is hot upon us, we jog on, and forget the immensity of this scheme of things.

44

The processes of Nature seem to be jesuitical.

There are workmen who do not suffer so much from the wages of sin as from the sin of low wages.

There are vanities and pretensions beyond laughter.

A well-bred person carries etiquette into his dreams, and displays *savoir vivre* even in sleep.

We may have been put into this world to be tested whether we will be honest in the dark.

Generally men die with their eyes open, as if staring for the way.

The Angel of Life tries to keep us out of our graves. And yet those who shall dig them are already alive and the linen of our grave clothes is spun.

Christ was crucified looking towards the West, and it is remarkable that it is in the West, not in the East, that His doctrine has triumphed.

45

The direct pursuit of Pleasure is a tactical error. The perfume of a rose seems to be stronger if the flower is held at a slight distance.

We agree that a man who is physically stronger than another is a coward if he takes advantage of his superiority. Should, therefore, a man who is intellectually stronger take a similar advantage?

There is no suffering more acute than the suffering of a well-bred person who happens to have made some slight blunder in etiquette.

Most men turn round at the sound of money when it falls.

There is a noticeable withdrawal among the crowd just before the hat is sent round.

Light, like the sea, moves in tides. The universe is iridescent.

There is in human life a most violent juxtaposition of the tragic and the comic.

I confess to a profound sense of Death. In any gay assembly I invariably reflect that in a few years we shall all have plunged underground.

The vast machinery of the universe, working throughout the night of ages, appears to exist for the sake of its own vibration.

There has never been any great thinker who has not passed through Gethsemane.

Patience is a kind of benignant shackles of the mind, and adversity a benignant poison.

The fundamental problem for all serious minds lies in the ethics of corruption.

Voltaire made extraordinary mistakes in literary criticism. For instance, he says of Corneille, "Je respecte beaucoup plus, sans doute, ce tragique français que le Grec." Now, *le Grec* was Sophocles!

47

Many persons desire the *entrée* when all that they can ever obtain is the exit.

Romance is the pious lie of the Imagination, and is a belief in "the good old times" which never existed.

It is marvellous to think that nothing really perishes, and that the wind which blows to-day may have filled the sails of Ulysses.

Wit is the light baggage of the mind.

Baudelaire seems to have had a moth - eaten brain.

The danger of depreciating your talent is that people take you at your word.

Thin lips are recognised as a sign of good breeding, and yet many apes have extremely thin lips.

It seems that nothing is really unimportant. An archæologist is able to reconstruct an entire historical period by the discovery of the middens of the Lake Dwellers.

Only jewels seem to have perpetual youth.

A jewel is a kind of permanent blossom.

There is something repulsive in the character of Cortes. Once his pilot disobeyed him. Cortes knew that the man was indispensable, and therefore he did not kill him, but he punished him by cutting off his feet.

Hate takes up too much room in the soul, and is a rowdy tenant.

In almost every heart there are great arrears of charity.

Some human eyes are so keen that they seem to vivisect all that they look upon.

Jugend ist Trunkenheit ohne Wein.

It is not necessary to cultivate the Ego, which is a bacillus that cultivates itself and requires no special nourishment.

Now and again it is well to regard our own destiny with the indifference with which other people regard it.

When we wish to express the nothingness of human life we say it is dust, but gunpowder is dust.

It was Villena who first used the exquisite phrase, " Gay Science."

The Inquisition was really an attack upon Property.

It should never be forgotten that Christianity has also produced monsters.   Torquemada.

Petrarch gave his lyrics and sonnets as alms to ballad mongers, and supposed that his fame would rest upon his Latin Epic, which the world has forgotten.   It is another instance of the fact that an author never sees his own work from the standpoint of the public.

Since vice undoubtedly destroys human Beauty, the moral consciousness is indirectly of *æsthetic* value.

A great Religion should not levy blackmail on the human race.

Those who are genuinely religious desire that Religion should be purged of bluff.

The Age of Chivalry was in reality false and vulgar. Courtesy and humane treatment were reserved only for those among the enemy who happened to be of gentle birth. The peasant and the common soldier were treated with remorseless cruelty, as, for instance, at the capture of Ruvo by Gonsalvo of Cordova. The Age of Chivalry begins with the noble line, " A man's a man for a' that."

Nelson said, " Get close, and you shall be victor."

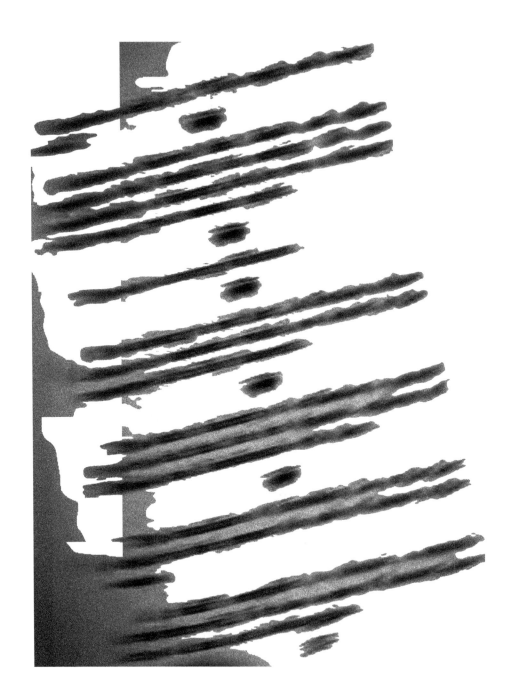

... should compromise implies a certain amount ... ..., but since the weakness is on both ... the result of the negotiations is an equivalence ...

The persecution of the Huguenots was a ...ful thing because it took this form: ← If ... ., your own property shall remain ... Otherwise, not."

Some persons are more just to their enemies ... to their friends.

It is more important to remain friends with ... ..lf than with others.

There is an extraordinary saying by Sir Thomas ......: " In brief, we are all monsters."

In this battle of life every living thing presses ... whole armour closer.

How full the soul is of the shadows and sim- .... of this world.

Columbus called it, " This rough and weary world."

Columbus believed that Isaiah and other prophets had foretold his coming. He was undoubtedly a visionary, but he was a visionary with maps, great seaman mystic. .

The sea is a moving wilderness.

It is amusing to read that La Fontaine, whose *Contes* are somewhat wicked, was buried in the cemetery of the Holy Innocents.

The latent barbarity of civilisation is proved by the fact that the first Spanish explorers of Florida took bloodhounds with them.

The foundation of friendship lies in the fact that for both persons the code of honour is the same.

A bailiff compelled to distrain a woman's furniture will, if he has a sense of humour, leave her at least one looking-glass.

No doubt compromise implies a certain amount of weakness, but since the weakness is on both sides the result of the negotiations is an equivalence of interests.

The persecution of the Huguenots was a frightful thing because it took this form: "If you recant, your own property shall remain yours. Otherwise, not."

Some persons are more just to their enemies than to their friends.

It is more important to remain friends with oneself than with others.

There is an extraordinary saying by Sir Thomas Browne: "In brief, we are all monsters."

In this battle of life every living thing presses its whole armour closer.

There is an image of a pot.

How full the soul is of the shadows and simulacra of this world.

Petrarch says of Fame, "È un echo, un sogno, anzi d'un sogno un' ombra."

One form of the immortal illusion is that the universe exists for man.

It is unfortunate that religion as soon as it is organised begins to display the characteristics of a syndicate, and implies vested interests.

Another form of the immortal illusion is that the Future has the keys of happiness. For most men well-being is perpetually adjourned. But the Future shall be like the Past, full of accidents.

The Paradox of the Ideal is this: There is no Ideal which as soon as reached does not vanish into another. We are able to discover no single end which can satisfy us, but only an accumulation of ends, that is to say, a process. But how can a process be an end in itself? A process is only a means. An end which becomes static is only a form of ennui. An Ideal that is content with itself, stagnant and otiose, loses the name of Ideal altogether. As soon as even the highest

54

condition has been realised new needs have begun
to accumulate. We are driven to the next stage
and to the next, until we become aware that
apparently the Ideal is not an object but a search
and a journey, a journey which is interminable,
in other words, a journey which is irrational, since
all journeys should end some time. If the result
of a journey is not an end in itself, how can the
journey be? We move from limit to limit, and
it is because consciousness of a limit implies
consciousness of what lies beyond the limit, as
Spinoza said, that it is no place to remain at,
but only a place in which to grow restive. The
old god Terminus, the god of boundaries, was
the vainest of all mythical creations, since the
hunger for new frontiers is never appeased.

It is difficult to find a common ground of
discussion with those who say that our system
of knowledge does not hold good in another
part of the universe. It is the only system of
knowledge which they and we possess. And
if ultimate ideas are to be intelligible they must
come into the scheme we know, the scheme of
antinomy and change. Whether, therefore,
reality be natural or supernatural it is all one.
We can know it only if it puts itself in relation
with the apparatus of knowledge with which we

are blessed or cursed. If we remove the foundations of human knowledge, which consist in a judgment of comparison and the sense of time, there is nothing more to be said.

As much "design" appears to have been spent on the creation of deadly organisms as on the creation of more beneficent things. There is no case in which a species works voluntarily for the sake of another.

If a horse be given the bedding which has already been used for some wild animal in a menagerie, he will be suddenly filled with terror, and will endeavour to break away. What a suggestion of the war of species!

According to Kant, there is in us an irresponsible instinct. It is a strange admission by one who allows some freedom to the will.

Kant points out that the vices of civilisation are the worst of all.

56

In Thebes there was a law which punished the representation of deformity.

Pleasure and Pain travel along the same nerve.

It is an interesting question why Rome had scarcely any tragic drama, and the answer probably is that it was a tradition of Roman character to repress the emotions.

The spirit of ridicule seems to be necessary for the progress of the world. Many an evil belief, such as witchcraft, has been laughed out of existence.

Almost all mistakes leave a mark and are irremediable. After confession, and in spite of it, in ridicule of it, the weight of the burden is doubled.

No sooner does a thing exist than its imitation and caricature begin to exist.

Now and again there is a strange fascination in the pageant of the world, and it was felt by Sir Thomas Browne when he said the world is

57

"courtly and splendid." It comes upon us sumptuous and scarlet—

"Wi' its hundred pipers an' a', an' a."

For most women life is a prolonged bazaar.

The most dangerous moment for an individual is not when others doubt about him but when he has doubts about himself.

There are those who make friends with the humble *in case* Scripture be fulfilled and the humble shall be exalted.

How could we prize wisdom unless there were fools?

The roses wither but not their thorns.

When we ask some intellectual person for his opinion regarding the mystery of existence, it is like one beggar begging from another.

Health means synthesis; disease is a sort of furious analysis ending in dissolution.

Love is feudalistic.

Faith often fits a new convert like ready-made clothes. One must grow with one's beliefs.

A man like Danton is capable of kindness to individuals, but is cruel when dealing with men *en masse*. He said, "I looked my crime steadfastly in the face, and committed it."

The frightful blot on the French Revolution consists in the fact that moderation was considered a crime.

Mirabeau said of the Revolution, "If women do not mix in it there will be nothing done."

Socialism is the worst of all tyrannies because it is anonymous.

A certain admiration cannot be withheld from the vigour of such phrases as Marat's: "Cailloux destinés à lapider des scélérats!"

A one day's gnat may feel life intolerably long.

What is called the unity of things is at present known only as a totality of contradictions.

The doctrine of resignation is more suited to age than to youth.

Criticism that is not also creative is bad criticism.

Opinion moves in epidemics.

The wavering barrier which separates a medicine from a poison, the minute additions or subtractions which cause the one to become the other, are matters of great interest to a speculative mind. Some of the names of poisons are as old as sorcery, and were invented in the night of human learning. Such names are *atropa bella donna* and *solanum*. It was an audacious thing

60

for the human mind to attempt to sift what was safe from what was dangerous in Nature. She is penetrated by poisons, and many of her tissues are drenched in them. In the mysterious economy of life they play an indispensable part, and work alternately towards construction and dissolution. Poison is a kind of secret nihilism of Nature.

The primary cause of probably every disease is a fact of profound significance. Invariably disease begins in the attempt of a single cell to set itself up independently of the rest, with the result that all its neighbours become its prey. The benign feudalism of health, in which all the members of the community obey a central control, disappears in disease, which is a form of cellular anarchy. In short, it is in the egoism of cellular life that disease springs.

The world is so full of interest that it is as difficult for the mind to distribute its allegiance to the various kinds of knowledge as it is for a Roman Catholic to distribute his devotion among his saints.

Prophecy appears to be the naïve expression of the doctrine of Necessity.

Dull people possess an extraordinary power of causing even brilliant persons who are long in their company to become likewise dull.

It is a startling fact that insanity increased rapidly among the black population after they were emancipated.

Why should Freedom be supposed to belong only to the Will? Why should not Desire be free?

The only haunted house is the human soul.

There are milestones on life's road, but they contradict each other, and their information is effaced by the weather.

Opportunism appears to be the only ethical system which the world has really adopted.

Pain is carnivorous.

Rigid Tories are persons who have only deductive habits of mind, and they continue to reason from principles which may have become stagnant.

All government, no matter by what name it is known, is in the hands of a few individuals. For although in a Democracy a plebiscite may be taken in order to discover whether, for instance, war should be declared, yet events may have been already precipitated by the acts of the half-dozen individuals who are managing the State. The temperament of an Ambassador or of a Minister, his method of expressing himself in a despatch, may be the cause of the excitement in public opinion, and the situation has been created not by the many but by the one. This is the revenge the aristocratic principle takes upon Democracy.

There is a kind of education by means of which we are not brought up but brought down.

The comic dramatists should never produce indignation but only derision in the audience; yet there are some of them who succeed in producing both.

Lessing's view that Pleasure should be the aim of the Fine Arts is seen to be incontrovertible if it is expressed negatively. For who could believe that the aim of the Fine Arts should be Pain? Tragedy is thus in a somewhat doubtful position.

A smile is more infectious than a frown.

Some persons who lend us their assistance are like those ink erasers which only make the blot worse.

Envy appears to be the actual spirit of robbery, but not bold enough to commit the theft.

The charity of certain persons is so ostentatious that it resembles a cruel hand exploring a wound.

The curse of great cities is that they destroy the horizon.

At the sight of great poverty riches appear to be a kind of blasphemy.

64

The immoral book is the book which hides Truth and creates a Fool's Paradise.

The difference between the realist and the idealist is that the one uses microscopes and the other telescopes.

When we lift the edge of the mask from the face of Life we discover a face of sorrow.

Ennui may be necessary for the sake of the economy of our forces.

It is strange that although we are allowed to plagiarise a man's moral qualities we dare not appropriate the things of his intellect.

Sometimes the best choice is not to choose at all.

We distinguish Fact from Fiction, but even in science it is hard to know where the one ends and the other begins.

Too much suspicion of human nature indicates as great ignorance of the world as too much confidence.

Comedy pretends that the world is not tragic, and Tragedy pretends it is not comic.

Optimism is the *mauvaise plaisanterie* of Philosophy.

Optimism is the dance music of philosophers. But above it, beneath it, drowning it, we hear the grunts and snarls of the real world.

The Romantic School is the great *Bon Marché* of Literature. Like Optimism, it is a concession to the desire for bazaars and bargains.

So far as ceremonies are concerned, all religions tend to become operatic.

There is something morbid, stifling, and horrible in Gothic architecture. It is like an illuminated hearse. During the Middle Ages the foundation stone of each cathedral was actually bathed in blood. The whole edifice belongs to Moloch. The windows are the colour of blood and ecchymosis. Hope does not dwell in those dreadful buildings, and the soul is oppressed by them. They are gigantic coffins and nothing more.

The soul is like a piece of metal distracted by too many magnets.

Love, like the wind, is both guider and misguider.

It is the hard task of the soul to avoid extremes, and to guide itself along a kind of weary diagonal.

There is no chaos which is not in process of becoming a cosmos, nor any cosmos which is not in process of becoming a chaos.

It is a strange spectacle when the soul opens the Book of Wisdom too late and reads it *illuminated* in hell.

So-called moral judgments finally pass into pathological judgments if the mind that makes them possesses any real insight into cause and effect.

The newspapers are mirrors which public personages take up every day in expectation of discovering their own reflection and in order to carry on the elaborate toilet of their reputation.

It is probably a moment of genuine suffering when a celebrated person perceives that his celebrity is diminishing. The crisis arrives when he visits the waxworks, and discovers that his wax figure, which used to delight the public, has been withdrawn. He infers that the wax has been melted down for a new model.

Sir Thomas Browne said, " The world to me is but a dream and mock show."

Optimists who undertake to soothe the soul by extracting its ills resemble those charlatans who advertise "painless dentistry." But the wary are not deceived.

68

"Klopfte man an die Gräber und fragte die Toten, ob sie wieder aufstehen wollten: sie würden mit den Köpfen schütteln."

In society it is more important to have a polished boot than a polished brain.

There is a strange paradox that certain fruit trees if planted in too rich soil become barren.

Asceticism is the invigorating winter among the seasons of the soul.

The most intellectual persons are those who make their wills serve their intellects, not their intellects their wills.

We should open our doors and windows to Laughter.

There is an excellent Italian proverb: "Non è così tristo cane che non mena la coda"—"There is no dog so miserable that he does not wag his tail."

Liquor and all artificial irritants should be expensive. The trouble is, however, that cheap imitations are invariably produced, and are even more harmful.

The perpetual desire for stimulus is a sign of poverty and vulgarity of soul.

We must browse where we are tethered.

The beginning of love is marked by a persistent use of the superlative degree, which, however, gradually gives way to the comparative and then to the positive, until the end is reached in the monosyllables of disillusion.

Our dreams are a kind of criticism of our lives and their *reductio ad absurdum.*

Too often the type is a blasphemy of the archetype.

Nothing sounds so false and nauseous as belated rapture.

It is with the passions as with certain plants and flowers. They will not grow outside a hotbed.

The real excitement begins when Reason is mixed with Love.

One good friend is better than all the clubs.

We should wear a mask for our pride's sake even although the soul is raging and sorrowing.

Marriage is only the after-vibration of love.

It was Montaigne who used the noble words: " I esteem all men my countrymen."

In great Tragedy there is something seismic. The movement is *molar*, that is to say, it is a movement of passion in masses. In Comedy the movement is *molecular.*

A great writer in poverty is compelled to gamble with his ideas.

When a cold, passionless person sits in judgment on his passionate fellow-creature, it is as if the Arctic regions were to object to the existence of the Tropics.

The sense of Beauty appears to require a repetition of instances, and passes from type to type. So far as the relations of the sexes are concerned, this fact produces calamitous results.

The Divorce Court is the dissecting-room of marriage.

The thistledown develops strange pricks.

In the whole physiology of love in its wane there is nothing so disreputable as the smile which simulates an ecstasy that has already vanished.

Repentance is the sickbed of the soul.

Nature has the aspect of a colossal gamble, because all birth is an interminable experiment in which millions of individuals perish for the sake of a few survivals.

A kind of mysticism lies at the back of almost every mind which has seriously thought about the universe. It may even be discovered co-existing with a style of thought in fundamental contradiction with it, as in the case of Pascal. It is the twilight and penumbra of thought, and marks the point at which the buffeted intellect has stopped. Who, indeed, will venture to say what lies in the unexplored backwoods of Knowledge?

Destiny has all the stars to gamble with.

Death is such an universal principle that for all we know there are graves in the stars.

Death is such an universal principle that for all we know there are graves in the stars.

The soul has to carry on its work in temporary premises.

Life shall be fatal to us unless we are able to find some pleasure in our own character.

Love is not merely romantic; it is necromantic.

Religion should be something more than a desire for gratuities hereafter on an immense scale.

A criticism of life should be as kaleidoscopic as life is.

Since all that we love and touch contains its own death-warrant and veiled corpse we are all necrophilists.

In Nature the central fact is restlessness.

The only command which has been thoroughly and joyfully obeyed is, "Be fruitful and multiply."

Intellectual cowardice is quite as disreputable as physical cowardice.

Moral feeling involves the dramatisation of consciousness.

Egoism is the determination of the individual to reserve the loud pedal for his own tunes and the soft pedal for the tunes of his rivals.

Faith is a kind of eavesdropping on the Unseen.

Saint Augustine believed that life is "a monstrous paradox."

The history of authors and critics resembles those processions of the Flagellants in which each man flogged the back of the man immediately in front of him.

No sooner does some obscure genius kindle a genuine fire of truth or of beauty than there is immediately formed a bucket brigade to prevent the flames from spreading.

A man who has done some good deeds has the satisfaction of the lamplighter when he turns round and sees that all his lamps are burning.

L'homme est de glace aux vérités;
Il est de feu pour les mensonges.

75

The peculiarity of "enlightened self-interest" is that it has a darkening effect on the interests of other people.

There are certain persons who, when compelled to praise those whom they dislike, make use of the soft pedal at its full capacity.

When love becomes passion etiquette perishes.

De la Rochefoucauld has a wonderful definition of love: "Il est difficile de définir l'amour: ce qu'on en peut dire est que, dans l'âme, c'est une passion de régner; dans les esprits, c'est une sympathie; et dans le corps, ce n'est qu'une envie cachée et délicate de posséder ce que l'on aime, après beaucoup de mystères."

Time and sorrow write their names upon the human face in italics.

We may murder Truth, but its wild, angry ghost will haunt and occupy the soul, and in vain will we cry to it, "Never shake thy gory locks at me!"

If the great passions could assume a visible shape their faces would be haggard.

In the history of mankind wisdom occupies only a footnote.

Those who are conscious that their reputation is waning should have the wisdom to withdraw altogether, since a reputation at half-mast, like a flag, is worse than none.

The beauty of jewels is that although they are ripe they can never be rotten.

The world is full of spurious friendships founded on the materialistic basis of barter.

What we call Fate is probably only a form of gravitation.

Millionaires are few, but millionaires in ideas are still fewer.

Mexicans, who are great horsemen, say that it is not enough for a man to know how to ride. He must know how to fall.

Like a hypochondriac, a jealous lover has always his finger on the pulse of love.

The idealist inhabits the future tense even although it be unfurnished.

The work of Baudelaire and of Poe appears to have the illumination of nightmare. But great art should not be haggard.

A man's pretension is the scaffold on which he perishes.

George Fox said, "Keep to Yea and Nay."

Apparently great men are permitted to dispense with certain acquirements which ordinary individuals are compelled to possess if they wish to avoid ridicule. Yet Chateaubriand gives an amusing explanation of the illegibility of Napoleon's handwriting. Napoleon wrote in an illegible manner in order to conceal the fact that he was unable to spell correctly.

The best definition of the Revolution is André Chénier's, " Stagnante Anarchie."

Ultimately all things come to pass, even the things that are reasonable.

Thought is a diver, but when it regains the surface its report is only that it has found the Deep deepening.

According to Campanella, evil is the tendency to non-existence.

In marriage the contracting parties tacitly guarantee the permanence of their moods. But who in his right senses can guarantee the permanence of anything, far less the permanence of his moods?

The danger of marriage is that after the first drunkenness of love is over the two beings may discover each other's characters to be bristling with irrelevancies. At first, love makes no scrutiny of the deeper things of character, takes character for granted, and, in short, is the solvent of all contradictions. Later, however, the chemical affinities may become so exhausted that the acids are left to begin their work of mutual destruction.

Gossip is tolerable only if it is good-natured.

Ultimate religious doctrines are the hiero-glyphics understood by no man.

The amazing complexity of Nature is best seen in Embryology. It seems that Embryologists have good reason to believe that every cell of the body contains in microscopic form such substances and properties as, under favourable conditions, would make it capable of developing into a complete human being.

Nature has no interest in anything except success. Her test of fitness is not moral. She is a workshop for the manufacture of deadly weapons, and she provides every organism with the means of pillage and aggression. Optimists forget this inarticulate crime of things.

80

Who can say that the processes of Nature are always beautiful ? There is a midge whose cells at a certain stage of their development begin to prey upon the body which is their common parent, devour it, leave it a heap of waste products, and issue from the débris to become in turn victims of the same strange method of propagation. There are numerous organisms in Nature gyrating like infernal machines.

We should train our minds in the rapid ⤳ mobilisation of ideas.

In the first shock of great disillusion the soul seems to suffer a kind of moral hæmorrhage.

A bee which uses its sting at its utmost capacity often dies as a result.

Self-love is the worst form of auto-intoxication.

One reason why the world turns away from Philosophers is that they have banished the discussion of love from their books. A few wise men, however, like Socrates and Schopenhauer, have shown that no Philosophy is complete until it has analysed love, which is the basis of human society.

Immersed in the exploitation of the world under our feet, we lose the sense of the firmament.

In a ballroom, " Am I pleasing? Am I pleasing? " is written on every face.

Often the most successful people are in need of the greatest consolation.

In the case of almost all of us there is a great gulf fixed between pretension and achievement.

Many men use up their talents in perpetual rehearsals of a drama that is never acted.

Philistinism is the beef-essence of ignorance. But it is not the naïve, delightful ignorance of the peasant, that ignorance of the world's affairs which almost amounts to a kind of negative

82

wisdom. The Philistine is a person of full-blown judgments and invincible opinions. He is the caricature and ape of culture. All that he demands from Art is an exact imitation of the world as *he* perceives it. Philistinism is one of the incurable diseases.

The difficulties under which the real work of Art is produced are enormous. The man of science, the astronomer or the physicist, publishes his investigations, which are immediately judged by experts—that is to say, by a set of men who are more or less on his own intellectual level. But in the case of the artist and man of letters the only ultimate court of appeal is that shifting mass of sensations and prejudices which forms the public mind. The canons of public taste are like the rules of fashion : if they have any permanence at all, it is the permanence of recurring decimals. The history of Criticism is mainly the history of failure to recognise the best Art on its first appearance. There is not, and probably there never can be, in Art as there is in Science, a body of organised knowledge universally accepted as the touchstone of æsthetic value. And the reason seems to be that whereas Science is a matter of verification in which Method is rigorous and uniform, Art is a matter of temperament. Now temperaments are infinite, and therefore the laws of taste remain in a state of permanent confusion. We have been able to define the units of Science, and all men are agreed upon them. But we have not been able to define the unit of Art, which is Beauty, and a chaos of criticism is the result. The ultimate judgment of each individual concerning a work of art is either "I like it," or "I do not like it." It is doubtful if the principles of æsthetics can be demonstrated; at least they can never be made as certain as mathematics. There is no *Zoll-Verein* of Temperaments.

How, for instance, can we prove to those who disagree with us that *Paradise Lost* is a greater thing than Young's *Night Thoughts*, or that a portrait by Holbein is a greater thing than a portrait by Guido Reni? Of course, it might be possible to show that certain laws of construction may have been obeyed in one case and disobeyed in another. But the problem of taste is something more than the question of mere technical excellence. It is a subtle affair of emotions, and the enthusiastic beholder may never be able to give satisfactory reasons why certain works of art move him profoundly. Thus the problem of æsthetics becomes a still deeper problem of Psychology. Ultimately, all that may be said is often only this: Certain persons at a high level of culture are conscious that certain works of art satisfy their emotional needs and their hunger for beautiful expression. But the difficulty of the attempt to create any unity of opinion on matters of art consists in the fact that Philistines may discover in objects of lower æsthetic value an æsthetic emotion genuine as far as it goes. There is an admirable line of Blake: " Your heaven doors are my hell gates ! " and that is often as true in Art as in Theology.

The popular view of Art is that it is an imitation of outward things. It may be stated quite clearly, therefore, either that (1) Art is an imitation of outward reality, in which case it adds nothing new to the world, or (2) that it is not an imitation but a reconstruction. If the word "imitation" were fit to be used in any profound sense—in the sense, for instance, in which Taine uses it—we might be able to say that there is a link of connection between those two theories. But if Art is *only* imitation, it certainly deserves the condemnation Plato gave it. Because, who, if he had a choice between the reality and the counterfeit, would choose the counterfeit? The world would then become filled with a multitude

85

of useless things. Besides, the gift of mimicry is the least intellectual of all gifts, and it is safe to say that if Art were only mimicry, if it consisted in nothing but a sure eye and hand, then great diligence should make artists of all of us. A photograph would be more valuable than a picture, and æsthetic insight would be a matter of acquisition. And then, since there is only one way of imitating a thing, we could discover no difference in the work of artists. But is it true that an artistic problem is like a problem in mathematics, capable of only one solution? We know that two scientific men working on the same problem expect to produce the same result, and they have means of protecting their conclusions from being influenced by their personal idiosyncrasies, such as the difference of the rate of vision in astronomy. But in Art the personality of the worker cannot be thus effaced. As a matter of fact, the history of Art is the history of perpetual variations of method and design. It is notorious that the same subject has been treated in utterly different ways not merely by different men but by the same man in different moods. Yet if the imitative theory be true, this difference should not exist. The " David " of Michael Angelo is not the " David " of Donatello. " The Last Supper " has been treated in a hundred different ways. A

Crucifixion by Van Dyck is utterly different from a Crucifixion by Tintoretto. No doubt the Academy at Siena is full of work done by a set of men who were content to efface their own personalities in order to obey the principles of their school. Except in the case of the two great leaders of that school, Tiepolo and Bazzi, hardly a picture is signed. The disciples attempted to produce, in their combined work, a single effect by imposing on the same subjects an unvarying treatment. But although we are impressed by their modesty we are not impressed by their power. The great artist is conscious of energies and conceptions of his own to which the subject in hand gives merely the starting-point. The *Faust* of Goethe is not the *Faust* of Marlowe. Besides, if it be true that Art which does not mimic experience is bad, then we shall have to surrender the dramas of Shakespeare and of Victor Hugo, because in ordinary experience men do not address each other as they do in those plays in rhymed couplets or blank verse. So that the best drama would be the shorthand report of a criminal trial. But the drama has assumed various forms throughout its history, and in spite of their dissimilarity we accept them all. Even if we look into the Volk songs of European nations, where if anywhere (because of the rudimentary nature of the emotion expressed)

87

we should expect to hear the same voice in the
same tone, we actually discover a deep psychological difference between, for instance, the Volk
songs of Venice and the Ballads of Scotland. It is
precisely from the death of Augustine in the fifth
century till the time of Sordello, a period half
covered by the Troubadours and the Trouveres,
when European poetry was absolutely uniform, and
when all the poets were saying the same thing in
the same way—it is just then that we find little
significance in what they said, and no prominent
names. If, finally, we consider that in music there
is not one way but that there are a thousand ways
of expressing an emotion, and that Beethoven's
music, which would have seemed monstrous to the
Greeks, is of profound significance to the modern
world, we begin to see that Art is something
more complex than imitation. In other words,
Art is in some way an interference with reality, or
it is reality seen through a temperament. Thus
all criticism is chiefly engaged either in defending
or attacking different kinds of temperaments.

The imitative theory of Art is more deeply
rooted in our minds than we are willing to admit.
It is at variance, however, with those profounder
views which have been expressed by all the great
modern writers who have discussed the nature of

beauty. According to Goethe, the function of Art is the expression of the characteristic. This definition, indeed, is the foundation of modern æsthetics. But the definition is so wide that it includes many things which at first sight appear scarcely to belong to Art. It means not merely that Art should reproduce the symmetrical beauty of the world, but that Life's whole "dramatic depth," whether ugly or beautiful, is the province of Art. The paradox of æsthetics consists in the fact that beauty and ugliness are relative conceptions, and that the one exists because the other exists. The darker side of Nature has even allured many great minds, and has found expression in the work of such men as Æschylus, Dante, Da Vinci, Goya, and Shakespeare. All the forces of Nature which threaten the well-being of man lend themselves to great imaginative expression. The Beautiful is sometimes the Terrible—*das schöne Shreckliche*. And so, too, in the inner world of the soul. The hazards of existence, the reawakening after illusion, the pathos of human things, the cries of oppression and disaster that are infinite in the world, are the stuff of which a great human Art is made. But such a treatment of Life, this gigantic element of the greatest Art, finds little response in ordinary existence. The great public turns away in terror from Art in which the realities of the world are made more real by imaginative expression.

Bad Art moves in the plane of sensations, great Art in the plane of emotions.

In all the calculations of life hope is the recurring decimal.

Egoism is mistaken policy, because it converts the whole world into an opponent.

Any old priest who recalls the *tête-à-tête* of the Confessional in which he may have sat for years probably finds that those dialogues keep living in his memory. His mind is now full of the débris of strange suggestion in the accumulated mass of which there take place new permutations and combinations of innumerable moral anarchies. Thought, and especially the darker kind of it, has a strange vitality and duration, and lingers like a perfume round the walls of the mind. It was probably such a reflection as this which caused Machiavelli in one of his plays (*Mandragola*) to write the following words: "Questi frati son trincati, astuti, ed è ragionevole, perchè e' sanno i peccati nostri, e' loro."

The soul is too much like a sponge, and absorbs unconsciously the elements in which it is immersed.

The books of a great writer are only a kind of paper money representing the mint of his brain.

In every active mind there is a perpetual immigration and emigration of ideas.

Love is an epidemic always raging.

Applause is like sea - water. The more we drink the thirstier we become.

The desire for fame is the attempt to lay up treasure for ourselves in the memories of men. But sooner or later those memories are full of the moths of oblivion.

With the lapse of time tombstones fall and lie prone, like the beings they commemorate. The ultimate posture of all things is horizontal.

The soul appears to suffer at the hands of Destiny a kind of violent *massage*, yet this may be necessary for its health.

It is doubtful whether the majority of Christians obey the exhortation to pray for each other. But they are occasionally observed preying *upon* each other.

Gratuitous services are sometimes very expensive.

In Science progress is collective. Each investigator is partaker in a combined advance, and achievement is heritable. In Art, however, owing to the irregular nature of genius, it is otherwise. In spite of "Schools," the movement is far more one of units at long intervals.

It is said that although we have sounded the hollowness of our own illusions we should still live for the sake of other people. Undoubtedly. But for what purpose? To increase their pleasures? That is, to increase their illusions. A few wise men, of whom Aristotle was one, have warned us that wisdom consists not in the attempt to procure pleasure but only the absence of pain. The more intense the pleasure the more frightful its loss. It is, therefore, doubtful whether we should make children intensely happy. The shock of real life shall produce a dangerous awakening. There is a kind of optimism which is actually evil and hurtful. Teachers who delude youth as to the real nature of the world are, therefore, like those dishonest packers of fruit who place all the best fruit on the top.

Fate is the head-wind that is always blowing.

The keen, rarefied air of the Ideal produces in certain persons a kind of mountain sickness.

The upper frosts and snows of the summit of the Ideal are not to be conquered in dancing slippers.

The human soul is a palimpsest of stigmata.

Near gold mines the land is always sterile.

93

Many of the judgments of this book may be contradictory. It is not possible for the human mind to reach a judgment in which the confusion of its moods and the multitudinous aspects of reality may be harmonised. The ultimate judgment is an affirmation of the danger of all judgments. For instance, everyone agrees that a barren tract in the midst of a fertile prairie is valueless. Yet if the prairie is on fire, the barren tract instantly becomes of the greatest value, because it impedes the progress of the fire. Almost all judgments suffer a perpetual process of subtraction and addition.

Fourier's attempt to discover the law of gravitation of the passions was doomed to failure. The "harmony of the passions" does not exist, because, like the inmates of a madhouse, the passions are incapable of combination.

The Maréchal de Saxe said, "Une bataille perdue, c'est une bataille qu'on croit perdue."

The real nature of the world is best seen in such calculations as Barot made regarding the

94

years of peace and the years of war. He found that from the fifteenth century B.C. till the middle of the nineteenth century A.D. there have been 227 years of peace and 3130 years of war. Moreover, while 8397 Treaties of Peace were sworn to be sacred for ever, their average duration was two years.

The second-rate is the main source of Comedy.

There is a remarkable touch of irony in the Book of Job, and it appears to indicate that its author must have been a married man. It is narrated that Satan deprived Job of every one and of every thing that could comfort him. He left him his wife.

The difference between Comedy and Tragedy is that Comedy causes the centre of gravity to become the centre of hilarity.

Rabelais puts an amusing question: *Qui feut premier, soif ou beuverye?*

95

A secret long kept becomes like an itch.

The universe is so vast that every star is only a parish in it.

Love, like the gulf stream, has a double current, hot and cold.

Death may be as refreshing as sleep.

Woe to the man whose luxuries have become necessities.

Nature has made some things so elusive and vast that they are incapable of being annexed, and are beyond the reach of aggression—light, the air, and the sea.

The triumph of the spirit of the world is seen in the manner in which religious symbols gradually lose their meaning and are converted into trinkets of worldly distinction. For instance, the Cross is set in diamonds and placed on the breasts of successful diplomatists, generals, and bankers. But there were no diamonds on the Cross of Christ.

Likewise, the manner in which religious festivals degenerate into actual feasts and become the occasion for the display of *haute cuisine* is remarkable. Christmas involves immense activity in the kitchens of Europe. Moreover, at Easter the modern world plants the Cross on its hot cross buns.

Real forgiveness comes only from those who are in love with us, and they grant it only because for the moment they are dazzled.

A woman in despair about her beauty goes from mirror to mirror.

There is a strange analogy between the fertility of error and the fertility of the lowest organisms in Nature. Not the highest but the lowest organisms are the most prolific. Ephemeroids propagate in millions. So, too, in the region of human opinion. The history of mankind teaches us that whereas the breeding power of Error is immense, Truth and Justice increase with intolerable delay.

Ibn Khaldun says that nobility in any family lasts only four generations. According to him, real nobility, at least among the Arabs, consisted not merely in the feeling of leadership, but "in the feeling for the community." He seems to mean that the altruistic sense gradually becomes exhausted, and that the patent of real nobility dies on the reappearance of a devouring egoism. This is a remarkable message from the North African deserts in the fourteenth century.

The soul is the demand for beauty and the heroic.

Political economists deny the "intrinsic value" of things, and point out that the only real value is the "exchange value." In other words—

> "The value of a thing
> Is just as much as it will bring."

At first sight this is a disturbing truth when applied to the things of Art and of the soul. Nevertheless, there may be a profound sense in which the soul's real value can be expressed only in the terms of exchange. Otherwise how can it be intelligible? If it has no relations it ceases to have meaning. But if it has relations they must be expressed either as relations of superiority or of inferiority, or of equivalence. The soul, however, is incapable of stating its own equation. At least, it finds nothing in the markets of the world for which it can give itself in exchange. It is this search for its equivalent that gives meaning to religion and ethics.

Many persons are unable to endure the conviction of intellectual inferiority. Thus when asked whether they have read such and such a book, intellectual vanity compels them to say yes, although their demeanour indicates that they have not spoken the truth. This is an attempt to display a façade of knowledge behind which nothing exists.

Life is so extraordinarily theatrical that theatres appear to be superfluous.

Arguments are generally barren and always troublesome.

99

The sense of wonder is not sapped, but rather enriched and deepened, by the work of the understanding.

There is an elective affinity between genial Scepticism and genial Belief.

That there are doubtful and unexplored places in human destiny will probably be admitted by even the most rigorous dogmatist. The deepest minds become conscious of an overwhelming sense of disproportion between their nescience and their knowledge. The profoundest spirits are those who, like Sir Thomas Browne, " pursue their reason to an *O altitudo!* " Precision and clearness and full light seem to belong not even to the sphere of the senses. And beyond that sphere and the small map of human experience there lies a vast mapless tract. If we were able to summon Plato, and to show him all that Science has done, how she has discovered fundamental forces and has weighed the stars, it is nevertheless unlikely that we should be able to persuade him that the real problem has changed since he handled it. He would still tell us that we know only " the world of appearances."

Behind all knowledge is the dim region of nescience, where, if illumination does not cease, it is at least so reduced that scarcely the boldest moves out of the light with a firm foot. This is the point at which belief and unbelief collapse in the last effort of the mind. All theories, if pushed far enough back, come face to face with the phantasmagoria of the unknown. Knowledge changes and fades, and like a vesture may be folded up. We know little except the rotation of opinion.

Nemesis is a form of the Eternal.

In this frantic struggle for each other's purses we forget that we are in a radiant universe and under beckoning firmaments.

The soul is safe until it begins to undermine itself from within.

Mirrors are always interesting because we find *ourselves* in them.

Epictetus says that a wise man watches himself as he would watch a treacherous enemy.

The doctrine of Epictetus is extraordinarily pure. His wisdom is not the fruit of bitterness or disillusion, but is *a priori* and perfect. In Seneca, on the contrary, we detect a less genuine serenity. He was a man of the world, and reached wisdom after illusion. Marcus Aurelius probably knew the actual world better than either of them. Unlike Epictetus, he had tasted pomp, but unlike Seneca, he was uncorrupted. In Seneca there is still a sense of the unappeased and a certain whine. He uses Philosophy much as a man in a dark place whistles to himself because he is afraid.

To Nemesis belongs the immense region of anticlimax.

The Temple of Nemesis is shunned, but we are all compelled to sit there at least once in our lives.

At every stage of our journey we order fresh relays of the post horses of illusion.

The wise man frequently says Mass in the Temple of Nemesis.

❦

The parvenu, like the sinner, must be born again.

❦

Modern culture is too often a rage for the panoramic, and suffers from an overgrowth of merely descriptive literature. Reflection and the search for meaning are neglected. There is a desire for the biograph but not for the real biography of things.

❦

It is part of the tragedy and of the comedy of human life that in some form or other we are all at auction. The world buys us and sells us or rejects us, and there is no escape from the market. Even those for whom there are no bidders are compelled to sit there, objects of derision.

❦

Among cooks the following maxim is considered to be the beginning of wisdom: "He cooks badly who cooks quickly."

The attempt of a superior character to accommodate himself to one who is inferior, to endure him charitably, to consort with him and educate him, has often dangerous reactive effects. It is as if a great architect were to be compelled to adjust the scheme of a noble building to the squalid buildings already standing round the site.

Even when the soul is vibrating with new beliefs, every good man feels that there is still something sacred in the faith which he was taught at his mother's knee.

Death may be migration.

The will is the surgeon of the soul.

What matters it to the wind whether the dust be of diamonds or of gold?

Even when the soul is loosening from its moorings there is probably no absolute unbelief, but there is abundant misbelief.

Poison often goes *incognito*, and is sweet to the taste.

Youth is the period of mingled aurora and mystery.

The sensitive face of a lover is the dial on which Love casts the shadow of his hours.

Love is the High Mass of the spirit.

We smile at the quarrels of children, because we know that the matter in dispute is trivial. Perhaps a higher order of beings smile at the quarrels of mankind and at the strife of nations.

The astute person is he who contrives in all the undertakings of life to secure a position near the exit.

Among snobs the entrance of a person of title is felt to be equivalent to the moment of the *elevation of the Host.*

Instead of acting on the maxim, "Il faut se retirer pour mieux sauter," cowards act on this inversion of it, *Il faut sauter pour se retirer mieux.*

There is perhaps no more remarkable proof of the fact that human things are for ever suffering change than the Preface which Marot wrote to the Poems of Villon. Marot points out that Villon's language had already become obsolete. But Marot's own language, in which that criticism is made, has become almost as obsolete as Villon's.

Si ne craings rien qui plus m'assaille
Car à la mort tout assouvyst.

Like all great writers, Villon expresses his thought with extreme verbal economy. For instance, he gives us in six little words the entire mediæval belief regarding the destiny of sinners after death—*Corps pourriz, et âmes en flammes.*

At death the soul is Outward-bound.

Religion is the startling rumour that there is another world.

❦

Almost every religious belief is a *cul-de-sac* for the intellect.

❦

The scheme of existence is such that to think about it persistently is to bring melancholy into the soul.

❦

Philosophy is one of the dangerous occupations because, although it may not imperil life or limb, ·it imperils our gaiety.

❦

The moral value of a great national crisis lies in the fact that the individual is compelled to merge and to forget his own interests in the larger interests of the State, and is thus moment- arily delivered from the paltry and maddening burden of the *self.*

❦

Husband, wife, and child are the triple expansion engines which keep humanity moving.

The male sex trust that the world accepts " bachelor " as equivalent to " virgin."

107

Cynicism is truth at freezing point.

Passion is the unexpurgated edition of Love.

Fancies and sentiments have rootlets, but the passions have roots.

The Real is only the Cartoon of the Ideal.

If it were true that Nature is never cruel, always beneficent, then, but only then, realism would be blasphemy.

It is almost terrifying to think that the universe which we see is only a detail in a vaster universe which we cannot see.

Every form of life and of energy is merely a phase in the *duration* of change. Empires and stars are episodes, and the entire universe is only an episode in the eternal metamorphosis.

Tertullian said that it belongs to Truth to laugh because Truth is gay. But this statement is only a delightful lie.

Le malheur fait les philosophes.

There are some cases in which a vice is so organic that its amputation would involve the death of the patient.

The unknown is the screen upon which we throw the images of our hopes and fears.

Aristotle defines man as a political animal. He is at least often an impolitic one.

Verbosity is tolerable only in love-letters.

Every cheque issued by the egoist reads " Pay to self."

Good literary style has the quality of a *still* wine. The sparkling wines end by fatiguing the palate.

The most incurable of all moral diseases is
the inflammation of the ego.

❦

Of all so-called Pagan philosophers Epictetus
appears to have delivered the doctrine which
has most practical value for the modern world.
And the reason probably is that, whereas other
teachers, like Socrates, entangled their moral
systems in a theory of knowledge, Epictetus—
at least in the form in which Arrianus has made
him known to us — concentrated his entire
criticism on the question of conduct. Intellectual
theories perish or grow obsolete far more rapidly
than systems of ethics or of belief. And the
main lines of human conduct were fixed long
before science or history began to give an account
of them. It would therefore be no exaggeration
to say that since the date of Epictetus hardly
any moral discoveries have been made. The
intellectual far more than the moral world is the
region of spiritual novelties. For instance, the
Church honoured herself by adopting the *En-
cheiridion* of Epictetus as a religious work, and
the message of that work is as fresh to-day as
when it was delivered at Nicopolis. It is remarkable that the great teachers of antiquity
wrote few books. Some of them, like Epictetus

and Socrates, wrote none. Their immense authority over their contemporaries was the result rather of conduct than of doctrine, and a man whose life was impressive became the founder of a school. Thus it was with Epictetus. So far as outward and worldly accomplishments were concerned, he was only poorly equipped. Great gifts of utterance and of persuasion he must have undoubtedly possessed, but he can have had no ready‑made passport to authority. Although little is known of him, it is at least authentic that he had been a slave. His master was Epaphroditus, the friend of Nero, and the imitator of Nero's cruelty. It is said that one day, in order to amuse himself, he broke Epictetus' leg. And it is at least probable that such a master made many attempts to test the Stoicism of such a slave. In any case, Epictetus appears to have come unscathed through all ordeals, and doubtless his suffering was the foundation of his wisdom. At what date he obtained his freedom we are ignorant, but it was probably later than 94 A.D. That was the year in which the Emperor Domitian expelled the philosophers from Rome, and thereafter we hear of Epictetus teaching at Nicopolis. He was surrounded by a group of disciples, chief among whom was Arrianus, to whom we owe the preservation of the main doctrines of the master.

Those doctrines are of the simplest kind. Every line of them is packed with value. Indeed, there is no ethical conception so simple or so impressive as the central thought of Epictetus. It is this—Some things are in our power; other things are not in our power. The things which are not in our power are the opinions of other people, the chances and the disasters of life; all, indeed, which lies outside of the soul—fame, fortune, and death. But the things which are in our power are the inward states of the will, —not events, but our opinion of events; not fortune, but our use and abuse of fortune; not death, but our fear of it. If, however, this be true, then good and evil exist not in events, or fortunes, or misfortunes, but "in a certain disposition of the will." This is the foundation of the entire Stoic doctrine. "What, then," asks Epictetus, "are outward events? Matter for the will, about which, being occupied, it shall attain its own good or evil. . . . If these things be true (and if we are not fools or hypocrites), good lies in the will, and likewise evil, and all other things are nothing to us. Why, then, are we troubled?" Now those words, if their meaning be grasped, should lift a weight off every mind which is stunned by the tumult of existence. So far from involving apathy or indifference, they imply a perpetual inner activity. At first it may be hard to believe that even the most disastrous event cannot harm us, but only our opinion of the event; yet the longer we reflect the truer this strange doctrine appears. For what is the task of the soul? It cannot regulate outward events, but only its own attitude towards them. Its success, therefore, its peace, must invariably come from its own inner states. Perhaps both Epictetus and Marcus Aurelius appear at first sight to neglect and belittle the keenness of human sensibility. The human organism is even dangerously responsive to every vibration of the outer world, and its responsiveness is part of its equipment. The rôle which imagination and illusion play in the mind is hardly considered by the Stoics. Epictetus tests a man's wisdom by his "use of appearances." He holds tenaciously to the great doctrine that "the things which are not in our power" can neither menace us nor disturb us. Any other doctrine is fatal to peace. "Outward things are not in my power; to will is in my power. But of all that is alien to thee, call nothing good, or evil, nor profitable, nor hurtful, nor any such term as these." In other words, the multitude of events are nothing in themselves, and have importance only as material for the will to work upon. Epictetus uses an image which is intensely Greek, for he says that "Life is like a game of ball. Now, this is what

you shall see done by skilful ball players. None
careth for the ball, as it were a thing good or
bad, but only about throwing it and catching
it. . . . And so should we do also, having the
carefulness of the most zealous players, and yet
indifference, as it were, merely about a ball." In
order to be understood, Epictetus must be accepted as a companion, and no more valuable
comrade ever offered himself to mankind. It
may be said that modern problems cannot be
solved by ancient methods. Modern life is
apparently more complex, the horizon is wider
and perhaps darker, duties have been multiplied,
and the entire scale and scheme of things is
different, because it is vaster. Nevertheless, if
we strip modern civilisation of its artificial com-
plexities and superfluities, we shall rediscover the
same problem of conduct which is laid bare
in the pages of Epictetus. At a stroke he
solves it. "Things are indifferent, but the
uses of them are not indifferent. My use of
the event is either evil or good, and this is in
my power."

Certain beliefs are like great stars which appear
and disappear and reappear in the long intervals
of their orbits.

The critic is the sick-nurse of Literature.

There is a point of view from which the Ideal is a moral danger. In so far as it is allowed to remain a fixed type it becomes a barrier, and the negation of movement.

At every moment the soul, consciously or not, is plunging in the Infinite.

One of those great sayings which make the heart beat faster is Proudhon's, "Liberté, c'est richesse, c'est noblesse."

If the history of the world were represented in a diagram it would be an extraordinary zigzag.

I think to-night of all the immense, dark prisons raised throughout the world like a kind of collective tombs full of living Humanity.

The shock of Life has come upon each of us in a different way. If, therefore, every mind were able to discover its own epigram, that is to say, the most vivid expression of its own experience, we should possess a wonderful collection of opinion on the meaning of Life.

Printed by MORRISON & GIBB LIMITED, *Edinburgh*

A CATALOGUE OF BOOKS PUBLISHED BY METHUEN AND COMPANY: LONDON 36 ESSEX STREET W.C.

CONTENTS

MARCH 1905

A CATALOGUE OF

MESSRS. METHUEN'S
PUBLICATIONS

Colonial Editions are published of all Messrs. METHUEN's Novels issued at a price above 2s. 6d., and similar editions are published of some works of General Literature. These are marked in the Catalogue. Colonial editions are only for circulation in the British Colonies and India.

An asterisk denotes that a book in the Press.

PART I.—GENERAL LITERATURE

Abbot (Jacob). See Little Blue Books.

Acatos (M. J.), Modern Language Master at King Edward School, Birmingham. See Junior School Books.

Adams (Frank). J C SPRATT. With 24 Coloured Pictures. *Super Royal 16mo.* 2s.

Adeney (W. F.), M.A. See Bennett and Adeney.

Æschylus. See Classical Translations.

Æsop. See Illustrated Pocket Library.

Ainsworth (W. Harrison). See Illustrated Pocket Library.

*Alderson (J. P.). MR. ASQUITH. With Portraits and Illustrations. *Demy 8vo.* 7s. 6d. net.

Alexander (William), D.D., Archbishop of Armagh. THOUGHTS AND COUNSELS OF MANY YEARS. Selected by J. H. BURN, B.D. *Demy 16mo.* 2s. 6d.

Alken (Henry). THE NATIONAL SPORTS OF GREAT BRITAIN. With descriptions in English and French: With 51 Coloured Plates. *Royal Folio. Five Guineas net.* See Illustrated Pocket Library.

Allen (Jessie). See Little Books on Art.

Allen (J. Romilly), F.S.A. See Antiquary's Books.

Almack (E.). See Little Books on Art.

Amherst (Lady). A SKETCH OF EGYPTIAN HISTORY FROM THE EARLIEST TIMES TO THE PRESENT DAY. With many Illustrations, some of which are in Colour. *Demy 8vo.* 10s. 6d. net.

Anderson (F. M.). THE STORY OF THE BRITISH EMPIRE FOR CHILDREN With many Illustrations. *Crown 8vo.* 2s.

Andrewes (Bishop). PRECES PRIVATAE. Edited, with Notes, by F. E. BRIGHTMAN, M.A., of Pusey House, Oxford. *Crown 8vo.* 6s.

Aristophanes. THE FROGS. Translated into English by E. W. HUNTINGFORD, M.A., Professor of Classics in Trinity College, Toronto. *Crown 8vo.* 2s. 6d.

Aristotle. THE NICOMACHEAN ETHICS. Edited, with an Introduction and Notes, by JOHN BURNET, M.A., Professor of Greek at St. Andrews. *Demy 8vo.* 10s. 6d. net.

Ashton (R.). See Little Blue Books.

Atkins (H. G.). See Oxford Biographies.

Atkinson (C. M.). JEREMY BENTHAM. *Crown 8vo.* 5s. A biography of this great thinker, and an estimate of his work and influence.

Atkinson (T. D.). A SHORT HISTORY OF ENGLISH ARCHITECTURE. With over 200 Illustrations by the Author and others. *Fcap. 8vo.* 3s. 6d. net.

Aurelius (Marcus). See Methuen's Universal Library.

Austen (Jane). See Little Library and Methuen's Universal Library.

Aves (Ernest). See Books on Business.

Bacon (Francis). See Little Library and Methuen's Universal Library.

Baden-Powell (R. S. S.), Major-General. THE DOWNFALL OF PREMPEH. A Diary of Life in Ashanti, 1895. With 21 Illustrations and a Map. *Third Edition. Large Crown 8vo.* 6s. A Colonial Edition is also published.

THE MATABELE CAMPAIGN, 1896. With nearly 100 Illustrations. *Fourth and Cheaper Edition. Large Crown 8vo. 6s.*
A Colonial Edition is also published.

Baker (W. G.), M.A. See Junior Examination Series.

Baker (Julian L.), F.I.C., F.C.S. See Books on Business.

Balfour (Graham). THE LIFE OF ROBERT LOUIS STEVENSON. *Second Edition. Two Volumes. Demy 8vo. 25s. net.*
A Colonial Edition is also published.

Bally (S. E.). See Commercial Series.

Banks (Elizabeth L.). THE AUTOBIOGRAPHY OF A 'NEWSPAPER GIRL. With a Portrait of the Author and her Dog. *Second Edition. Crown 8vo. 6s.*
A Colonial Edition is also published.

Barham (R. H.). See Little Library.

Baring-Gould (S.). Author of 'Mehalah,' etc. THE LIFE OF NAPOLEON BONA- PARTE. With over 450 Illustrations in the Text, and 12 Photogravure Plates. *Gilt top. Large quarto. 36s.*

THE TRAGEDY OF THE CÆSARS. With numerous Illustrations from Busts, Gems, Cameos, etc. *Fifth Edition. Royal 8vo. 10s. 6d. net.*

A BOOK OF FAIRY TALES. With numerous Illustrations and Initial Letters by ARTHUR J. GASKIN. *Second Edition. Crown 8vo. Buckram. 6s.*

A BOOK OF BRITTANY. With numerous Illustrations. *Crown 8vo. 6s.*
Uniform in scope and size with Mr. Baring-Gould's well-known books on Devon, Cornwall, and Dartmoor.

OLD ENGLISH FAIRY TALES. With numerous Illustrations by F. D. BEDFORD. *Second Edition. Crown 8vo. Buckram. 6s.*
A Colonial Edition is also published.

THE VICAR OF MORWENSTOW: A Biography. A new and Revised Edition. With a Portrait. *Crown 8vo. 3s. 6d.*
A completely new edition of the well-known biography of R. S. Hawker.

DARTMOOR: A Descriptive and Historical Sketch. With Plans and numerous Illustra- tions. *Crown 8vo. 6s.*

THE BOOK OF THE WEST. With numerous Illustrations. *Two volumes.* Vol. I. Devon. *Second Edition.* Vol. II. Cornwall. *Second Edition. Crown 8vo. 6s. each.*

A BOOK OF NORTH WALES. With numerous Illustrations. *Crown 8vo. 6s.*
This book is uniform with Mr. Baring-Gould's books on Devon, Dartmoor, and Brittany.

*A BOOK OF SOUTH WALES. With many Illustrations. *Crown 8vo. 6s.*

A BOOK OF GHOSTS. With 8 Illustrations by D. Murray Smith. *Second Edition. Crown 8vo. 6s.*
A Colonial Edition is also published.

OLD COUNTRY LIFE. With 67 Illustrations. *Fifth Edition. Large Crown 8vo. 6s.*

*AN OLD ENGLISH HOME. With numerous Plans and Illustrations. *Cr. 8vo. 2s. 6d. net.*

*YORKSHIRE ODDITIES AND STRANGE EVENTS. *Fifth Edition. Crown 8vo. 2s. 6d. net.*

*STRANGE SURVIVALS AND SUPERSTITIONS. *Third Edition. Cr. 8vo. 2s. 6d. net.*
A Colonial Edition is also published.

A GARLAND OF COUNTRY SONG: English Folk Songs with their Traditional Melodies. Collected and arranged by S. BARING-GOULD and H. F. SHEPPARD. *Demy 4to. 6s.*

SONGS OF THE WEST: Traditional Ballads and Songs of the West of England, with their Melodies. Collected by S. BARING-GOULD, M.A., and H. F. SHEPPARD, M.A. In 4 Parts. *Parts I., II., III., 2s. 6d. each. Part IV., 4s. In One Volume, French Morocco, 10s. net.; Roan, 15s.*
See also The Little Guides.

Barker (Aldred F.), Author of 'Pattern Analysis,' etc. See Textbooks of Technology.

Barnes (W. E.), D.D., Hulsaean Professor of Divinity at Cambridge. See Churchman's Bible.

Barnett (Mrs. P. A.). See Little Library.

Baron (R. R. N.), M.A. FRENCH PROSE COMPOSITION. *Crown 8vo. 2s. 6d. Key, 3s. net.* See also Junior School Books.

Barron (H. M.), M.A., Wadham College, Oxford. TEXTS FOR SERMONS. With a Preface by Canon SCOTT HOLLAND. *Crown 8vo. 3s. 6d.*

Bastable (C. F.), M.A., Professor of Economics at Trinity College, Dublin. See Social Questions Series.

Batson (Mrs. Stephen). A BOOK OF THE COUNTRY AND THE GARDEN. Illustrated by F. CARRUTHERS GOULD and A. C. GOULD. *Demy 8vo. 10s. 6d.*

A CONCISE HANDBOOK OF GARDEN FLOWERS. *Fcap. 8vo. 3s. 6d.*

*Batten (Loring W.), Ph.D., S.T.D., Rector of St. Mark's Church, New York; sometime Professor in the Philadelphia Divinity School. THE HEBREW PROPHET. *Crown 8vo.* 3s. 6d. net.

Beaman (A. Hulme). PONS ASINORUM; OR, A GUIDE TO BRIDGE. *Second Edition. Fcap. 8vo.* 2s.

Beard (W. S.). See Junior Examination Series.
EASY EXERCISES IN ARITHMETIC. Arranged by. *Cr. 8vo.* Without Answers, 1s. With Answers, 1s. 3d.

Beckford (Peter). THOUGHTS ON HUNTING. Edited by J. OTHO PAGET, and Illustrated by G. H. JALLAND. *Second and Cheaper Edition. Demy 8vo.* 6s.

Beckford (William). See Little Library.

Beeching (H. C.), M.A., Canon of Westminster. See Library of Devotion.

Behmen (Jacob). THE SUPERSENSUAL LIFE. Edited by BERNARD HOLLAND. *Fcap. 8vo.* 3s. 6d.

Belloc (Hilaire). PARIS. With Maps and Illustrations. *Crown 8vo.* 6s.

Bellot (H. H. L.), M.A. THE INNER AND MIDDLE TEMPLE. With numerous Illustrations. *Crown 8vo.* T 6s. net.
See also L. A. A. Jones.

Bennett (W. H.), M.A. A PRIMER OF THE BIBLE. *Second Edition. Crown 8vo.* 2s. 6d.

Bennett (W. H.) and Adeney (W. F.). A BIBLICAL INTRODUCTION. *Second Edition. Crown 8vo.* 7s. 6d.

Benson (Archbishop). GOD'S BOARD: Communion Addresses. *Fcap. 8vo.* 3s. 6d. net.

Benson (A. C.), M.A. See Oxford Biographies.

Benson (R. M.). THE WAY OF HOLINESS: a Devotional Commentary on the 110th Psalm. *Crown 8vo.* 5s.

Bernard (E. R.), M.A., Canon of Salisbury. THE ENGLISH SUNDAY. *Fcap. 8vo.* 1s. 6d.

Bertouch (Baroness de). THE LIFE OF FATHER IGNATIUS, O.S.B., THE MONK OF LLANTHONY. With Illustrations. *Demy 8vo.* 10s. 6d. net.
A Colonial Edition is also published.

Bethune-Baker (J. F.), M.A., Fellow of Pembroke College, Cambridge. See Handbooks of Theology.

Bidez (M.). See Byzantine Texts.

Biggs (C. R. D.), D.D. See Churchman's Bible.

Bindley (T. Herbert), B.D. THE OECUMENICAL DOCUMENTS OF THE FAITH. With Introductions and Notes. *Crown 8vo.* 6s.
A historical account of the Creeds.

Binyon (Laurence). THE DEATH OF ADAM, AND OTHER POEMS. *Crown 8vo.* 3s. 6d. net.

Birnstingl (Ethel). See Little Books on Art.

Blair (Robert). See Illustrated Pocket Library.

Blake (William). See Illustrated Pocket Library and Little Library.

Blaxland (B.), M.A. See Library of Devotion.

Bloom (T. Harvey), M.A. SHAKESPEARE'S GARDEN. With Illustrations. *Fcap. 8vo.* 3s. 6d. ; *leather.* 4s. 6d. net.

Blouet (Henri). See The Beginner's Books.

Boardman (T. H.). See Text Books of Technology.

Bodley (J. E. C.). Author of 'France.' THE CORONATION OF EDWARD VII. *Demy 8vo.* 21s. net. By Command of the King.

Body (George), D.D. THE SOUL'S PILGRIMAGE : Devotional Readings from his published and unpublished writings. Selected and arranged by J. H. BURN, B.D. F.R.S.E. *Pott 8vo.* 2s. 6d.

Bona (Cardinal). See Library of Devotion.

Boon (F. C.). See Commercial Series.

Borrow (George). See Little Library.

Bos (J. Ritzema). AGRICULTURAL ZOOLOGY. Translated by J. R. AINSWORTH DAVIS, M.A. With an Introduction by ELEANOR A. ORMEROD, F.E.S. With 155 Illustrations. *Crown 8vo. Third Edition.* 3s. 6d.

Botting (C. G.), B.A. EASY GREEK EXERCISES. *Crown 8vo.* 2s. See also Junior Examination Series.

Boulton (E. S.). GEOMETRY ON MODERN LINES. *Crown 8vo.* 2s.

Bowden (E. M.). THE IMITATION OF BUDDHA : Being Quotations from Buddhist Literature for each Day in the Year. *Fourth Edition. Crown 16mo.* 2s. 6d.

Boyle (W.). CHRISTMAS AT THE ZOO. With Verses by W. BOYLE and 24 Coloured Pictures by H. B. NEILSON. *Super Royal 16mo.* 2s.
Brabant (F. G.), M.A. See The Little Guides.
Brodrick (Mary) and Morton (Anderson). A CONCISE HANDBOOK OF EGYPTIAN ARCHÆOLOGY. With many Illustrations. *Crown 8vo.* 3s. 6d.
Brooke (A. S.), M.A. SLINGSBY AND SLINGSBY CASTLE. With many Illustrations. *Crown 8vo.* 7s. 6d.
Brooks (E. W.). See Byzantine Texts.
Brown (P. H.), Fraser Professor of Ancient (Scottish) History at the University of Edinburgh. SCOTLAND IN THE TIME OF QUEEN MARY. *Demy 8vo.* 7s. 6d. net.
Browne (Sir Thomas). See Methuen's Universal Library.
Brownell (C. L.). THE HEART OF JAPAN. Illustrated. *Third Edition. Crown 8vo.* 6s. ; also *Demy 8vo.* 6d.
  A Colonial Edition is also published.
Browning (Robert). See Little Library.
Buckland (Francis T.). CURIOSITIES OF NATURAL HISTORY. With Illustrations by HARRY B. NEILSON. *Crown 8vo.* 3s. 6d.
Buckton (A. M.). THE BURDEN OF ENGELA: a Ballad-Epic. *Third Edition. Crown 8vo.* 3s. 6d. net.
EAGER HEART: A Mystery Play. *Third Edition. Crown 8vo.* 1s. net.
Budge (E. A. Wallis). THE GODS OF THE EGYPTIANS. With over 100 Coloured Plates and many Illustrations. *Two Volumes. Royal 8vo.* £3, 3s. net.
Bull (Paul), Army Chaplain. GOD AND OUR SOLDIERS. *Crown 8vo.* 6s.
  A Colonial Edition is also published.
Bulley (Miss). See Social Questions Series.
Bunyan (John). THE PILGRIM'S PROGRESS. Edited, with an Introduction, by C. H. FIRTH, M.A. With 39 Illustrations by R. ANNING BELL. *Cr. 8vo.* 6s. See also Library of Devotion and Methuen's Universal Library.
Burch (G. J.), M.A., F.R.S. A MANUAL OF ELECTRICAL SCIENCE. With numerous Illustrations. *Crown 8vo.* 3s.
Burgess (Gelett). GOOPS AND HOW TO BE THEM. With numerous Illustrations. *Small 4to.* 6s.
Burke (Edmund). See Methuen's Universal Library.
Burn (A. E.), D.D., Prebendary of Lichfield. See Handbooks of Theology.
Burn (J. H.), B.D. See Library of Devotion.
Burnand (Sir F. C.). RECORDS AND REMINISCENCES, PERSONAL AND GENERAL. With many Illustrations. *Demy 8vo. Two Volumes. Third Edition.* 25s. net.
  A Colonial Edition is also published.
Burns (Robert), THE POEMS OF. Edited by ANDREW LANG and W. A. CRAIGIE. With Portrait. *Third Edition. Demy 8vo, gilt top.* 6s.
Burnside (W. F.), M.A. OLD TESTAMENT HISTORY FOR USE IN SCHOOLS. *Crown 8vo.* 3s. 6d.
Burton (Alfred). See Illustrated Pocket Library.
Butler (Joseph). See Methuen's Universal Library.
Caldecott (Alfred), D.D. See Handbooks of Theology.
Calderwood (D. S.), Headmaster of the Normal School, Edinburgh. TEST CARDS IN EUCLID AND ALGEBRA. In three packets of 40, with Answers. 1s. each. Or in three Books, price 2d., 2d., and 3d.
Cambridge (Ada) [Mrs. Cross]. THIRTY YEARS IN AUSTRALIA. *Demy 8vo.* 7s. 6d.
  A Colonial Edition is also published.
Canning (George). See Little Library.
Capey (E. F. H.). See Oxford Biographies.
Careless (John). See Illustrated Pocket Library.
Carlyle (Thomas). THE FRENCH REVOLUTION. Edited by C. R. L. FLETCHER, Fellow of Magdalen College, Oxford. *Three Volumes. Crown 8vo.* 18s.
THE LIFE AND LETTERS OF OLIVER CROMWELL. With an Introduction by C. H. FIRTH, M.A., and Notes and Appendices by Mrs. S. C. LOMAS. *Three Volumes. Demy 8vo.* 18s. net.
Carlyle (R. M. and A. J.), M.A. See Leaders of Religion.
Chamberlin (Wilbur B.). ORDERED TO CHINA. *Crown 8vo.* 6s.
  A Colonial Edition is also published.
Channer (C. C.) and Roberts (M. E.). LACE-MAKING IN THE MIDLANDS, PAST AND PRESENT. With 16 full-page Illustrations. *Crown 8vo.* 2s. 6d.
Chatterton (Thomas). See Methuen's Universal Library.

Chesterfield (Lord), THE LETTERS OF, TO HIS SON. Edited, with an Introduction by C. STRACHEY, and Notes by A. CALTHROP. *Two Volumes.* *Cr. 8vo.* 12*s.*

Christian (F. W.) THE CAROLINE ISLANDS. With many Illustrations and Maps. *Demy 8vo.* 12*s. 6d. net.*

Cicero. See Classical Translations.

Clarke (F. A.), M.A. See Leaders of Religion.

Cleather (A. L.) and Crump (B.). RICHARD WAGNER'S MUSIC DRAMAS: Interpretations, embodying Wagner's own explanations. *In Four Volumes.* *Fcap 8vo.* 2*s. 6d. each.*

    VOL. I.—THE RING OF THE NIBELUNG.

    VOL. II.—PARSIFAL, LOHENGRIN, and THE HOLY GRAIL.

Clinch (G.) See The Little Guides.

Clough (W. T.), Head of the Physical Department East Ham Technical College. See Junior School Books.

Coast (W. G), B.A. EXAMINATION PAPERS IN VERGIL. *Crown 8vo.* 2*s.*

Cobb (T.). See Little Blue Books.

Collingwood (W. G.), M.A. THE LIFE OF JOHN RUSKIN. With Portraits. *Second and Cheap Edition.* *Cr. 8vo.* 6*s.* Also a Popular Edition. *Cr. 8vo.* 2*s. 6d. net.*

Collins (W. E.), M.A. See Churchman's Library.

Colonna. HYPNEROTOMACHIA POLIPHILI UBI HUMANA OMNIA NON NISI SOMNIUM ESSE DOCET ATQUE OBITER PLURIMA SCITU SANE QUAM DIGNA COMMEMORAT. An edition limited to 350 copies on handmade paper. *Folio. Three Guineas net.*

Combe (William). See Illustrated Pocket Library.

Cook (A. M.), M.A. See E. C. Marchant.

Cooke-Taylor (R. W.). See Social Questions Series.

Corelli (Marie). THE PASSING OF THE GREAT QUEEN: A Tribute to the Noble Life of Victoria Regina. *Small 4to.* 1*s.*

A CHRISTMAS GREETING. *Sm. 4to.* 1*s.*

Corkran (Alice). See Little Books on Art.

Cotes (Rosemary). DANTE'S GARDEN. With a Frontispiece. *Second Edition.* *Fcap. 8vo. cloth* 2*s. 6d.*; *leather,* 3*s. 6d. net.*

BIBLE FLOWERS. With a Frontispiece and Plan. *Fcap. 8vo.* 2*s. 6d. net.*

Cowley (Abraham). See Little Library.

Cox (J. Charles), LL.D., F.S.A. See Little Guides.

Cox (Harold), B.A. See Social Questions Series.

Crabbe (George). See Little Library.

Craigie (W. A.). A PRIMER OF BURNS. *Crown 8vo.* 2*s. 6d.*

Craik (Mrs.). See Little Library.

Crashaw (Richard). See Little Library.

Crawford (F. G.). See Mary C. Danson.

Crouch (W.). BRYAN KING. With a Portrait. *Crown 8vo.* 3*s. 6d. net.*

Cruikshank (G.) THE LOVING BALLAD OF LORD BATEMAN. With 11 Plates. *Crown 16mo.* 1*s. 6d. net.*

    From the edition published by C. Tilt, 1811.

Crump (B.). See A. L. Cleather.

Cunliffe (F. H. E.), Fellow of All Souls' College, Oxford. THE HISTORY OF THE BOER WAR. With many Illustrations, Plans, and Portraits. *In 2 vols.* *Quarto.* 15*s. each.*

Cutts (E. L.), D.D. See Leaders of Religion.

Daniell (G. W.), M.A. See Leaders of Religion.

Danson (Mary C.) and Crawford (F. G.). FATHERS IN THE FAITH. *Small 8vo.* 1*s. 6d.*

Dante. LA COMMEDIA DI DANTE. The Italian Text edited by PAGET TOYNBEE, M.A., D.Litt. *Crown 8vo.* 6*s.* See also Paget Toynbee, Little Library, and Methuen's Universal Library.

Darley (George). See Little Library.

Davenport (Cyril). See Connoisseur's Library and Little Books on Art.

Dawson (A. J.). MOROCCO. Being a bundle of jottings, notes, impressions, tales, and tributes. With many Illustrations. *Demy 8vo.* 10*s. 6d. net.*

Deane (A. C.). See Little Library.

Delbos (Leon). THE METRIC SYSTEM. *Crown 8vo.* 2*s.*

Demosthenes: THE OLYNTHIACS AND PHILIPPICS. Translated upon a new principle by OTHO HOLLAND *Crown 8vo.* 2*s. 6d.*

Demosthenes. AGAINST CONON AND CALLICLES. Edited with Notes and Vocabulary, by F. DARWIN SWIFT, M.A. *Fcap. 8vo.* 2s.

Dickens (Charles). See Illustrated Pocket Library.

Dickinson (Emily). POEMS. First Series. *Crown 8vo.* 4s. 6d. net.

Dickinson (G. L.), M.A., Fellow of King's College, Cambridge. THE GREEK VIEW OF LIFE. *Third Edition. Crown 8vo.* 2s. 6d.

Dickson (H. N.), F.R.S.E., F.R.Met. Soc. METEOROLOGY. Illustrated. *Crown 8vo.* 2s. 6d.

Dilke (Lady). See Social Questions Series.

Dillon (Edward). See Connoisseur's Library.

Ditchfield (P. H.), M.A., F.S.A. ENGLISH VILLAGES. Illustrated. *Crown 8vo.* 2s. 6d. net.

THE STORY OF OUR ENGLISH TOWNS. With an Introduction by AUGUSTUS JESSOPP, D.D. *Second Edition. Crown 8vo.* 6s.

OLD ENGLISH CUSTOMS: Extant at the Present Time. An Account of Local Observances, Festival Customs, and Ancient Ceremonies yet Surviving in Great Britain. *Crown 8vo.* 6s.

Dixon (W. M.), M.A. A PRIMER OF TENNYSON. *Second Edition. Crown 8vo.* 2s. 6d.

ENGLISH POETRY FROM BLAKE TO BROWNING. *Second Edition. Crown 8vo.* 2s. 6d.

Dole N. H.). FAMOUS COMPOSERS. With Portraits. *Two Volumes. Demy 8vo.* 12s. net.

Dowden (J.), D.D., Lord Bishop of Edinburgh. See Churchman's Library.

Drage (G.) See Books on Business.

Driver (S. R.), D.D., Canon of Christ Church, Regius Professor of Hebrew in the University of Oxford. SERMONS ON SUBJECTS CONNECTED WITH THE OLD TESTAMENT. *Crown 8vo.* 6s. See also Westminster Commentaries.

Dryhurst (A. R.). See Little Books on Art.

Duguid (Charles), City Editor of the *Morning Post*, Author of the 'Story of the Stock Exchange,' etc. See Books on Business.

Duncan (S. J.) (Mrs. COTES), Author of 'A Voyage of Consolation.' ON THE OTHER SIDE OF THE LATCH. *Second Edition. Crown 8vo.* 6s.

Dunn (J. T.), D.Sc., **and Mundella (V. A.).** GENERAL ELEMENTARY SCIENCE. With 114 Illustrations. *Crown 8vo.* 3s. 6d.

Dunstan (A. E.), B.Sc., Head of the Chemical Department, East Ham Technical College. See Junior School Books.

*Durham (The Earl of). A REPORT ON CANADA. With an Introductory Note. *Demy 8vo.* 4s. 6d. net.

Dutt (W. A.). A POPULAR GUIDE TO NORFOLK. *Medium 8vo.* 6d. net.

THE NORFOLK BROADS. With coloured and other Illustrations by FRANK SOUTHGATE. *Large Demy 8vo.* 21s. net. See also The Little Guides.

Earle (John), Bishop of Salisbury. MICROCOSMOGRAPHE, OR A PIECE OF THE WORLD DISCOVERED; IN ESSAYES AND CHARACTERS. *Post 16mo.* 2s net. Reprinted from the Sixth Edition published by Robert Allot in 1633.

Edwards (Clement). See Social Questions Series.

Edwards (W. Douglas). See Commercial Series.

*Edwards (Betham). HOME LIFE IN FRANCE. With many Illustrations. *Demy 8vo.* 7s. 6d. net.

Egan (Pierce). See Illustrated Pocket Library.

Egerton (H. E.), M.A. A HISTORY OF BRITISH COLONIAL POLICY. *Demy 8vo.* 12s. 6d.
A Colonial Edition is also published.

Ellaby (C. G.). See The Little Guides.

Ellerton (F. G.). See S. J. Stone.

Ellwood (Thomas), THE HISTORY OF THE LIFE OF. Edited by C. G. CRUMP, M.A. *Crown 8vo.* 6s.

Engel (E.). A HISTORY OF ENGLISH LITERATURE: From its Beginning to Tennyson. Translated from the German *Demy 8vo.* 7s. 6d. net.

Fairbrother (W. H.), M.A. THE PHILOSOPHY OF T. H. GREEN. *Second Edition. Crown 8vo.* 3s. 6d.

FELISSA; OR, THE LIFE AND OPINIONS OF A KITTEN OF SENTIMENT. With 12 Coloured Plates. *Post 16mo.* 2s. 6d. net. (5¼ × 3¾). From the edition published by J. Harris, 1811.

Farrer (Reginald). THE GARDEN OF ASIA. *Second Edition. Crown 8vo. 6s.*
A Colonial Edition is also published.
Ferrier (Susan). See Little Library.
Fidler (T. Claxton), M.Inst. C.E., Professor of Engineering, University College, Dundee in the University of St. Andrews. See Books on Business.
Fielding (Henry). See Methuen's Universal Library.
Finn (S. W.), M.A. See Junior Examination Series.
Firth (C. H.), M.A. CROMWELL'S ARMY: A History of the English Soldier during the Civil Wars, the Commonwealth, and the Protectorate. *Crown 8vo. 6s.*
Fisher (G. W.), M.A. ANNALS OF SHREWSBURY SCHOOL. With numerous Illustrations. *Demy 8vo. 10s. 6d.*
FitzGerald (Edward). THE RUB'AIYAT OF OMAR KHAYYÀM. Printed from the Fifth and last Edition. With a Commentary by Mrs. STEPHEN BATSON, and a Biography of Omar by E. D. Ross. *Crown 8vo. 6s.* See also Miniature Library.
Flecker (W. H.), M.A., D.C.L., Headmaster of the Dean Close School, Cheltenham. THE STUDENT'S PRAYER BOOK. Part I. MORNING AND EVENING PRAYER AND LITANY. With an Introduction and Notes. *Crown 8vo. 2s. 6d.*
Flux (A. W.), M.A., William Dow Professor of Political Economy in M'Gill University, Montreal: sometime Fellow of St. John's College, Cambridge, and formerly Stanley-Jevons Professor of Political Economy in the Owens Coll., Manchester. ECONOMIC PRINCIPLES. *Demy 8vo. 7s. 6d. net.*
Fortescue (Mrs. G.) See Little Books on Art.
Fraser (David). A MODERN CAMPAIGN; OR, WAR AND WIRELESS TELE-GRAPHY IN THE FAR EAST. Illustrated. *Crown 8vo. 6s.*
Fraser (J. F.). ROUND THE WORLD ON A WHEEL. With 100 Illustrations. *Third Edition. Crown 8vo. 6s.*
A Colonial Edition is also published.
French (W.). See Textbooks of Technology.
Freudenreich (Ed. von). DAIRY BACTERIOLOGY. A Short Manual for the Use of Students. Translated by J. R. AINSWORTH DAVIS, M.A. *Second Edition. Revised. Crown 8vo. 2s. 6d.*
Fulford (H. W.), M.A. See Churchman's Bible.
C. G., and F. C. G. JOHN BULL'S ADVENTURES IN THE FISCAL WONDER-LAND. By CHARLES GEAKE. With 46 Illustrations by F. CARRUTHERS GOULD. *Second Edition. Crown 8vo. 2s. 6d. net.*
Gallichan (W. M.). See The Little Guides.
Gambado (Geoffrey, Esq.). See Illustrated Pocket Library.
Gaskell (Mrs.). See Little Library.
Gasquet, the Right Rev. Abbot, O.S.B. See Antiquary's Books.
George (H. B.), M.A., Fellow of New College, Oxford. BATTLES OF ENGLISH HISTORY. With numerous Plans. *Fourth Edition.* Revised, with a new Chapter including the South African War. *Crown 8vo. 6s.*
A HISTORICAL GEOGRAPHY OF THE BRITISH EMPIRE. *Crown 8vo. 3s. 6d.*
Gibbins (H. de B.), Litt.D., M.A. INDUSTRY IN ENGLAND: HISTORICAL OUTLINES. With 5 Maps. *Third Edition. Demy 8vo. 10s. 6d.*
A COMPANION GERMAN GRAMMAR. *Crown 8vo. 1s. 6d.*
THE INDUSTRIAL HISTORY OF ENGLAND. *Tenth Edition.* Revised. With Maps and Plans. *Crown 8vo. 3s.*
ENGLISH SOCIAL REFORMERS. *Second Edition. Crown 8vo. 2s. 6d.*
See also Commercial Series and Social Questions Series.
Gibbon (Edward). THE DECLINE AND FALL OF THE ROMAN EMPIRE. A New Edition, edited with Notes, Appendices, and Maps, by J. B. BURY, M.A., Litt.D., Regius Professor of Greek at Cambridge. *In Seven Volumes. Demy 8vo. Gilt top, 8s. 6d. each.* Also, *Crown 8vo. 6s. each.*
MEMOIRS OF MY LIFE AND WRITINGS. Edited, with an Introduction and Notes, by G. BIRKBECK HILL, LL.D. *Crown 8vo. 6s.*
See also Methuen's Universal Library.
Gibson (E. C. S.), D.D., Vicar of Leeds. See Westminster Commentaries, Handbooks of Theology, and Oxford Biographies.
Gilbert (A. R.). See Little Books on Art.
Godfrey (Elizabeth). A BOOK OF REMEMBRANCE. *Fcap. 8vo. 2s. 6d. net.*
Godley (A. D.), M.A., Fellow of Magdalen College, Oxford. LYRA FRIVOLA. *Third Edition. Fcap. 8vo. 2s. 6d.*
VERSES TO ORDER. *Second Edition. Fcap. 8vo. 2s. 6d.*
SECOND STRINGS. *Fcap. 8vo. 2s. 6d.*

Goldsmith (Oliver). THE VICAR OF WAKEFIELD. With 24 Coloured Plates by T. ROWLANDSON. *Royal 8vo. One Guinea net.*
Reprinted from the edition of 1817. Also *Fcap. 32mo.* With 10 Plates in Photogravure by Tony Johannot. *Leather, 2s. 6d. net.* See also Illustrated Pocket Library and Methuen's Universal Library.

Goudge (H. L.), M.A., Principal of Wells Theological College. See Westminster Commentaries.

Graham (P. Anderson). See Social Questions Series.

Granger (F. S.), M.A., Litt.D. PSYCHOLOGY. *Second Edition. Crown 8vo. 2s. 6d.*
THE SOUL OF A CHRISTIAN. *Crown 8vo. 6s.*

Gray (E. M'Queen). GERMAN PASSAGES FOR UNSEEN TRANSLATION. *Crown 8vo. 2s. 6d.*

Gray (P. L.), B.Sc., formerly Lecturer in Physics in Mason University College, Birmingham. THE PRINCIPLES OF MAGNETISM AND ELECTRICITY: an Elementary Text-Book. With 181 Diagrams. *Crown 8vo. 3s. 6d.*

Green (G. Buckland), M.A., Assistant Master at Edinburgh Academy, late Fellow of St. John's College, Oxon. NOTES ON GREEK AND LATIN SYNTAX. *Crown 8vo. 3s. 6d.*

Green (E. T.), M.A. See Churchman's Library.

Greenidge (A. H. J.), M.A. A HISTORY OF ROME: During the Later Republic and the Early Principate. *In Six Volumes. Demy 8vo.* Vol. I. (133-104 B.C). *10s. 6d. net.*

Greenwell (Dora). See Miniature Library.

Gregory (R. A.) THE VAULT OF HEAVEN. A Popular Introduction to Astronomy. With numerous Illustrations. *Crown 8vo. 2s. 6d.*

Gregory (Miss E. C.). See Library of Devotion.

Greville Minor. A MODERN JOURNAL. Edited by J. A. SPENDER. *Crown 8vo. 3s. 6d. net.*

Grinling (C. H.). A HISTORY OF THE GREAT NORTHERN RAILWAY, 1845-95. With Illustrations. Revised, with an additional chapter. *Demy 8vo. 10s. 6d.*

Grubb (H. C.). See Textbooks of Technology.

Guiney (Louisa I.). HURRELL FROUDE: Memoranda and Comments. Illustrated. *Demy 8vo. 10s. 6d. net.*

Gwynn (M. L.). A BIRTHDAY BOOK. *Royal 8vo. 12s.*

Hackett (John), B.D. A HISTORY OF THE ORTHODOX CHURCH OF CYPRUS. With Maps and Illustrations. *Demy 8vo. 15s. net.*

Haddon (A. C.), Sc.D., F.R.S. HEAD-HUNTERS, BLACK, WHITE, AND BROWN. With many Illustrations and a Map. *Demy 8vo. 15s.*

Hadfield (R. A.). See Social Questions Series.

Hall (R. N.) and Neal (W. G.). THE ANCIENT RUINS OF RHODESIA. With numerous Illustrations. *Second Edition, revised. Demy 8vo. 10s. 6d. net.*

Hall (R. N.). GREAT ZIMBABWE. With numerous Plans and Illustrations. *Royal 8vo. 21s. net.*

Hamilton (F. J.), D.D. See Byzantine Texts.

Hammond (J. L.). CHARLES JAMES FOX: A Biographical Study. *Demy 8vo. 10s. 6d.*

Hannay (D.). A SHORT HISTORY OF THE ROYAL NAVY, FROM EARLY TIMES TO THE PRESENT DAY. Illustrated. *Two Volumes. Demy 8vo. 7s. 6d. each.* Vol. I. 1200-1688.

Hannay (James O.), M.A. THE SPIRIT AND ORIGIN OF CHRISTIAN MONASTICISM. *Crown 8vo. 6s.*
THE WISDOM OF THE DESERT. *Crown 8vo. 3s. 6d. net.*

Hare, (A. T.), M.A. THE CONSTRUCTION OF LARGE INDUCTION COILS. With numerous Diagrams. *Demy 8vo. 6s.*

Harrison (Clifford). READING AND READERS. *Fcap. 8vo. 2s. 6d.*

Hawthorne (Nathaniel). See Little Library.

HEALTH, WEALTH AND WISDOM. *Crown 8vo. 1s. net.*

Heath (Frank R.). See The Little Guides.

Heath (Dudley). See Connoisseur's Library.

Hello (Ernest). STUDIES IN SAINTSHIP. Translated from the French by V. M. CRAWFORD. *Fcap 8vo. 3s. 6d.*

Henderson (B. W.), Fellow of Exeter College, Oxford. THE LIFE AND PRINCIPATE OF THE EMPEROR NERO. With Illustrations. *Demy 8vo. 10s. 6d. net.*

Henderson (T. F.). See Little Library and Oxford Biographies.

Henley (W. E.). ENGLISH LYRICS. *Second Edition. Crown 8vo. 2s. 6d. net.*

Henley (W. E.) and Whibley (C.). A BOOK OF ENGLISH PROSE. *Crown 8vo. Buckram, gilt top. 6s.*

Henson (H. H.), B.D., Canon of Westminster. APOSTOLIC CHRISTIANITY: As Illustrated by the Epistles of St. Paul to the Corinthians. *Crown 8vo. 6s.*

A 2

LIGHT AND LEAVEN: HISTORICAL AND SOCIAL SERMONS. *Crown 8vo.* 6s.
DISCIPLINE AND LAW. *Fcap. 8vo.* 2s. 6d.
Herbert (George). See Library of Devotion.
Herbert of Cherbury (Lord). See Miniature Library.
Hewins (W. A. S.), B.A. ENGLISH TRADE AND FINANCE IN THE SEVEN-
TEENTH CENTURY. *Crown 8vo.* 2s. 6d.
Heywood (W.). PALIO AND PONTE: A Book of Tuscan Games. Illustrated.
Royal 8vo. 21s. *net.*
Hilbert (T.). See Little Blue Books.
Hill (Clare), Registered Teacher to the City and Guilds of London Institute. See Textbooks
of Technology.
Hill (Henry), B.A., Headmaster of the Boy's High School, Worcester, Cape Colony. A
SOUTH AFRICAN ARITHMETIC. *Crown 8vo.* 3s. 6d.
This book has been specially written for use in South African schools.
Hillegas (Howard C.). WITH THE BOER FORCES. With 24 Illustrations. *Second*
Edition. Crown 8vo. 6s.
Hobhouse (Emily). THE BRUNT OF THE WAR. With Map and Illustrations.
Crown 8vo. 6s.
A Colonial Edition is also published.
Hobhouse (L. T.), Fellow of C.C.C., Oxford. THE THEORY OF KNOWLEDGE.
Demy 8vo. 10s. 6d. *net.*
Hobson (J. A.), M.A. INTERNATIONAL TRADE: A Study of Economic Principles.
Crown 8vo. 2s. 6d. *net.* See also Social Questions Series.
Hodgkin (T.), D.C.L. See Leaders of Religion.
Hogg (Thomas Jefferson). SHELLEY AT OXFORD. With an Introduction by
R. A. STREATFEILD. *Fcap. 8vo.* 2s. *net.*
Holden-Stone (G. de). See Books on Business.
Holdich (Sir T. H.), K.C.I.E. THE INDIAN BORDERLAND: being a Personal
Record of Twenty Years. Illustrated. *Demy 8vo.* 10s. 6d. *net.*
Holdsworth (W. S.), M.A. A HISTORY OF ENGLISH LAW. *In Two Volumes.*
Vol. I. *Demy 8vo.* 10s. 6d. *net.*
Holyoake (G. J.). See Social Questions Series.
Hoppner. See Little Galleries.
Horace. See Classical Translations.
Horsburgh (E. L. S.), M.A. WATERLOO: A Narrative and Criticism. With Plans.
Second Edition. Crown 8vo. 5s. See also Oxford Biographies.
Horth (A. C.), Master of Art and Manual Training Departments, Roan School, Greenwich.
See Textbooks of Technology.
Horton (R. F.), D.D. See Leaders of Religion.
Hosie (Alexander). MANCHURIA. With Illustrations and a Map. *Second Edition.*
Demy 8vo. 7s. 6d. *net.*
How (F. D.). SIX GREAT SCHOOLMASTERS. With Portraits and Illustrations.
Demy 8vo. 7s. 6d.
Howell (G.). See Social Questions Series.
Hudson (Robert). MEMORIALS OF A WARWICKSHIRE VILLAGE. With many
Illustrations. *Demy 8vo.* 15s. *net.*
Hughes (C. E.). THE PRAISE OF SHAKESPEARE. An English Anthology. With
a Preface by SIDNEY LEE. *Demy 8vo.* 3s. 6d. *net.*
Hughes (Thomas). TOM BROWN'S SCHOOLDAYS. With an Introduction and
Notes by VERNON RENDALL. *Leather. Royal 32mo.* 2s. 6d. *net.*
Hutchinson (Horace G.). THE NEW FOREST. Described by. Illustrated in colour
with 50 Pictures by WALTER TYNDALE and 4 by Miss LUCY KEMP WELCH. *Large Demy*
8vo. 21s. *net.*
Hutton (A. W.), M.A. See Leaders of Religion.
Hutton (R. H.). See Leaders of Religion.
Hutton (W. H.), M.A. THE LIFE OF SIR THOMAS MORE. With Portraits.
Second Edition. Crown 8vo. 5s. See also Leaders of Religion.
Hyett (F. A.). A SHORT HISTORY OF FLORENCE. *Demy 8vo.* 7s. 6d. *net.*
Ibsen (Henrik). BRAND. A Drama. Translated by WILLIAM WILSON. *Third Edition.*
Crown 8vo. 3s. 6d.
Inge (W. R.), M.A., Fellow and Tutor of Hertford College, Oxford. CHRISTIAN MYS-
TICISM. The Bampton Lectures for 1899. *Demy 8vo.* 12s. 6d. *net.* See also Library of
Devotion.
Innes (A. D.), M.A. A HISTORY OF THE BRITISH IN INDIA. With Maps and
Plans. *Crown 8vo.* 6s.

Jackson (S.), M.A. See Commercial Series.
Jackson (F. Hamilton). See The Little Guides.
Jacob (F.), M.A. See Junior Examination Series.
Jeans (J. Stephen). See Social Questions Series.
Jeffreys (D. Gwyn). DOLLY'S THEATRICALS. Described and Illustrated with 24 Coloured Pictures. *Super Royal 16mo. 2s. 6d.*
Jenks (E.), M.A., Reader of Law in the University of Oxford. ENGLISH LOCAL GOVERNMENT. *Crown 8vo. 2s. 6d.*
Jessopp (Augustus), D.D. See Leaders of Religion.
Jevons (F. B.), M.A., Litt.D., Principal of Hatfield Hall, Durham. See Churchman's Library and Handbooks of Theology.
Johnson (Mrs. Barham). WILLIAM BODHAM DONNE AND HIS FRIENDS. With Illustrations. *Demy 8vo. 10s. 6d. net.*
Johnston (Sir H. H.), K.C.B. BRITISH CENTRAL AFRICA. With nearly 200 Illustrations and Six Maps. *Second Edition. Crown 4to. 18s. net.*
Jones (H.). See Commercial Series.
Jones (L. A. Atherley), K.C., M.P., and Bellot (Hugh H. L.). THE MINERS' GUIDE TO THE COAL MINES' REGULATION ACTS. *Crown 8vo. 2s. 6d. net.*
Jonson (Ben). See Methuen's Universal Library.
Julian (Lady) of Norwich. REVELATIONS OF DIVINE LOVE. Edited by GRACE WARRACK. *Crown 8vo. 3s. 6d.*
Juvenal. See Classical Translations.
Kaufmann (M.). See Social Questions Series.
Keating (J. F.), D.D. THE AGAPE AND THE EUCHARIST. *Crown 8vo. 3s. 6d.*
Keats (John). THE POEMS OF. Edited with Introduction and Notes by E. de Selincourt, M.A. *Demy 8vo. 7s. 6d. net.* See also Little Library and Methuen's Universal Library.
Keble (John). THE CHRISTIAN YEAR. With an Introduction and Notes by W. LOCK, D.D., Warden of Keble College. Illustrated by R. ANNING BELL. *Third Edition. Fcap. 8vo. 3s. 6d.; padded morocco, 5s.* See also Library of Devotion.
Kempis (Thomas à). THE IMITATION OF CHRIST. With an Introduction by DEAN FARRAR. Illustrated by C. M. GERE. *Third Edition. Fcap. 8vo. 3s. 6d.; padded morocco, 5s.* See also Library of Devotion and Methuen's Universal Library. Also Translated by C. BIGG, D.D. *Crown 8vo. 3s. 6d.*
Kennedy (James Houghton), D.D., Assistant Lecturer in Divinity in the University of Dublin. ST. PAUL'S SECOND AND THIRD EPISTLES TO THE CORINTHIANS. With Introduction, Dissertations and Notes. *Crown 8vo. 6s.*
Kestell (J. D.). THROUGH SHOT AND FLAME: Being the Adventures and Experiences of J. D. KESTELL, Chaplain to General Christian de Wet. *Crown 8vo. 6s.*
Kimmins (C. W.), M.A. THE CHEMISTRY OF LIFE AND HEALTH. Illustrated. *Crown 8vo. 2s. 6d.*
Kinglake (A. W.). See Little Library.
Kipling (Rudyard). BARRACK-ROOM BALLADS. *73rd Thousand. Cr. 8vo. Twentieth Edition. 6s.*
A Colonial Edition is also published.
THE SEVEN SEAS. *62nd Thousand. Ninth Edition. Crown 8vo, gilt top, 6s.*
A Colonial Edition is also published.
THE FIVE NATIONS. *41st Thousand. Second Edition. Crown 8vo. 6s.*
A Colonial Edition is also published.
DEPARTMENTAL DITTIES. *Sixteenth Edition. Crown 8vo. Buckram. 6s.*
A Colonial Edition is also published.
Knowling (R. J.), M.A., Professor of New Testament Exegesis at King's College, London. See Westminster Commentaries.
Lamb (Charles and Mary), THE WORKS OF. Edited by E. V. LUCAS. With Numerous Illustrations. *In Seven Volumes. Demy 8vo. 7s. 6d. each.*
THE ESSAYS OF ELIA. With over 100 Illustrations by A. GARTH JONES, and an Introduction by E. V. LUCAS. *Demy 8vo. 10s. 6d.*
THE KING AND QUEEN OF HEARTS: An 1805 Book for Children. Illustrated by WILLIAM MULREADY. A new edition, in facsimile, edited by E. V. LUCAS. *1s. 6d.*
See also Little Library.
Lambert (F. A. H.). See The Little Guides.
Lambros (Professor). See Byzantine Texts.
Lane-Poole (Stanley). A HISTORY OF EGYPT IN THE MIDDLE AGES. Fully Illustrated. *Crown 8vo. 6s.*

Langbridge (F.) M.A. BALLADS OF THE BRAVE: Poems of Chivalry, Enterprise, Courage, and Constancy. *Second Edition.* *Crown 8vo.* *2s. 6d.*

Law (William). See Library of Devotion.

Leach (Henry). THE DUKE OF DEVONSHIRE. A Biography. With 12 Illustrations. *Demy 8vo.* *12s. 6d. net.*
A Colonial Edition is also published.

*Lee (Captain L. Melville). A HISTORY OF POLICE IN ENGLAND. *Crown 8vo.* *3s. 6d. net.*

Leigh (Percival). THE COMIC ENGLISH GRAMMAR. Embellished with upwards of 50 characteristic Illustrations by JOHN LEECH. *Post 16mo.* *2s. 6d. net.*

Lewes (V.B.), M.A. AIR AND WATER. Illustrated. *Crown 8vo.* *2s. 6d.*

Lisle (Fortunée de). See Little Books on Art.

Littlehales (H.). See Antiquary's Books.

Lock (Walter), D.D., Warden of Keble College. ST. PAUL, THE MASTER-BUILDER. *Second Edition.* *Crown 8vo.* *3s. 6d.* See also Leaders of Religion.

Locke (John). See Methuen's Universal Library.

Locker (F.). See Little Library.

Longfellow (H. W.) See Little Library.

Lorimer (George Horace). LETTERS FROM A SELF-MADE MERCHANT TO HIS SON. *Twelfth Edition.* *Crown 8vo.* *6s.*
A Colonial Edition is also published.

OLD GORGON GRAHAM. *Second Edition.* *Crown 8vo.* *6s.*
A Colonial Edition is also published.

Lover (Samuel). See Illustrated Pocket Library

E. V. L. and C. L. G. ENGLAND DAY BY DAY: Or, The Englishman's Handbook to Efficiency. Illustrated by GEORGE MORROW. *Fourth Edition.* *Fcap. 4to.* *1s. net.*
A burlesque Year-Book and Almanac.

Lucas (E. V.). THE LIFE OF CHARLES LAMB. With numerous Portraits and Illustrations. *Two Vols.* *Demy 8vo.* *21s. net.*

Lucian. See Classical Translations.

Lyde (L. W.), M.A. See Commercial Series.

Lydon (Noel S.) See Junior School Books.

Lyttelton (Hon. Mrs. A.). WOMEN AND THEIR WORK. *Crown 8vo.* *2s. 6d.*

M. M. HOW TO DRESS AND WHAT TO WEAR. *Crown 8vo,* *1s. net.*

Macaulay (Lord). CRITICAL AND HISTORICAL ESSAYS. Edited by F. C. MONTAGUE, M.A. *Three Volumes.* *Cr. 8vo.* *18s.*
The only edition of this book completely annotated.

M'Allen (J. E. B.), M.A. See Commercial Series.

MacCulloch (J. A.). See Churchman's Library.

MacCunn (F.). See Leaders of Religion.

McDermott. (E. R.), Editor of the *Railway News,* City Editor of the *Daily News.* See Books on Business.

M'Dowall (A. S.). See Oxford Biographies.

Mackay (A. M.). See Churchman's Library.

Magnus (Laurie), M.A. A PRIMER OF WORDSWORTH. *Crown 8vo.* *2s. 6d.*

Mahaffy (J. P.), Litt.D. A HISTORY OF THE EGYPT OF THE PTOLEMIES. Fully Illustrated. *Crown 8vo.* *6s.*

Maitland (F. W.), LL.D., Downing Professor of the Laws of England in the University of Cambridge. CANON LAW IN ENGLAND. *Royal 8vo.* *7s. 6d.*

Malden (H. E.), M.A. ENGLISH RECORDS. A Companion to the History of England. *Crown 8vo.* *3s. 6d.*

THE ENGLISH CITIZEN: HIS RIGHTS AND DUTIES. *Crown 8vo.* *1s. 6d.*

Marchant (E. C.), M.A., Fellow of Peterhouse, Cambridge. A GREEK ANTHOLOGY. *Second Edition.* *Crown 8vo.* *3s. 6d.*

Marchant (E. C.), M.A., and **Cook (A. M.),** M.A. PASSAGES FOR UNSEEN TRANSLATION. *Second Edition.* *Crown 8vo.* *3s. 6d.*

Marlowe (Christopher). See Methuen's Universal Library.

Marr (J. E.), F.R.S., Fellow of St John's College, Cambridge. THE SCIENTIFIC STUDY OF SCENERY. *Second Edition.* Illustrated. *Crown 8vo.* *6s.*

AGRICULTURAL GEOLOGY. With numerous Illustrations. *Crown 8vo.* *6s.*

Marvell (Andrew). See Little Library.

Maskell (A.) See Connoisseur's Library.

Mason (A. J.), D.D. See Leaders of Religion.

Massee (George). THE EVOLUTION OF PLANT LIFE: Lower Forms. With Illustrations. *Crown 8vo.* *2s. 6d.*

Masterman (C. F. G.), M.A. TENNYSON AS A RELIGIOUS TEACHER. *Cr. 8vo.* ·6s.

May (Phil). THE PHIL MAY ALBUM. *Second Edition.* 4to. 1s. net.

Mellows (Emma S.). A SHORT STORY OF ENGLISH LITERATURE. *Crown 8vo.* 3s. 6d.

Michell (E. B). THE ART AND PRACTICE OF HAWKING. With 3 Photogravures by G. E. LODGE, and other Illustrations. *Demy 8vo.* 10s. 6d.

*****Millais (J. G.).** THE LIFE AND LETTERS OF SIR JOHN EVERETT MILLAIS, President of the Royal Academy. With 319 Illustrations, of which 9 are in Photogravure. *New Edition. Demy 8vo.* 7s. 6d. net.

Millais (Sir John Everett). See Little Galleries.

Millis (C. T.), M.I.M.E., Principal of the Borough Polytechnic College. See Textbooks of Technology.

Milne (J. G.), M.A. A HISTORY OF ROMAN EGYPT. Fully Illustrated. *Crown 8vo.* 6s.

Milton, John, THE POEMS OF, BOTH ENGLISH AND LATIN, Compos'd at several times. Printed by his true Copies.
The Songs were set in Musick by Mr. HENRY LAWES, Gentleman of the Kings Chappel, and one of His Majesties Private Musick.
Printed and publish'd according to Order.
Printed by RUTH RAWORTH for HUMPHREY MOSELEY, and are to be sold at the signe of the Princes Armes in Pauls Churchyard, 1645.
See also Little Library and Methuen's Universal Library.

Minchin (H. C.), M.A. See Little Galleries.

Mitchell (P. Chalmers), M.A. OUTLINES OF BIOLOGY. Illustrated. *Second Edition. Crown 8vo.* 6s.
A text-book designed to cover the Schedule issued by the Royal College of Physicians and Surgeons.

'**Moil (A.).**' See Books on Business.

Moir (D. M.). See Little Library.

Moore (H. E.). See Social Questions Series.

Moran (Clarence G.). See Books on Business.

More (Sir Thomas). See Methuen's Universal Library.

Morfill (W. R.), Oriel College, Oxford. A HISTORY OF RUSSIA FROM PETER THE GREAT TO ALEXANDER II. With Maps and Plans. *Crown 8vo.* 3s. 6d.

Morich (R. J.), late of Cl' ton College. See School Examination Series.

Morris (J. E.). See The Little Guides.

Morton (Miss Anderson). See Miss Brodrick.

Moule (H. C. G.), D.D., Lord Bishop of Durham. See Leaders of Religion.

Muir (M. M. Pattison), M.A. THE CHEMISTRY OF FIRE. The Elementary Principles of Chemistry. Illustrated. *Crown 8vo.* 2s. 6d.

Mundella (V. A.), M.A. See J. T. Dunn.

Munro (R.), LL.D. See The Antiquary's Books.

Naval Officer (A). See Illustrated Pocket Library.

Neal (W. G.). See R. N. Hall.

Newman (J. H.) and others. See Library of Devotion.

Nichols (J. B. B.). See Little Library.

Nicklin (T.), M.A. EXAMINATION PAPERS IN THUCYDIDES. *Crown 8vo.* 2s.

Nimrod. See Illustrated Pocket Library.

Northcote (James), R.A. THE CONVERSATIONS OF JAMES NORTHCOTE, R.A., AND JAMES WARD. Edited by ERNEST FLETCHER. With many Portraits. *Demy 8vo* 10s. 6d.

*****Norway (A. H.)**, Author of 'Highways and Byways in Devon and Cornwall.' NAPLES. With 24 Coloured Illustrations by MAURICE GREIFFENHAGEN. A New Edition. *Crown 8vo. 6s.*

Novalis. THE DISCIPLES AT SAÏS AND OTHER FRAGMENTS. Edited by Miss UNA BIRCH. *Fcap. 8vo.* 3s. 6d.

Oliphant (Mrs.). See Leaders of Religion.

Oman (C. W. C.), M.A., Fellow of All Souls', Oxford. A HISTORY OF THE ART OF WAR. Vol. II.: The Middle Ages, from the Fourth to the Fourteenth Century. Illustrated. *Demy 8vo.* 10s. 6d net.

Ottley (R. L.), D.D., Professor of Pastoral Theology at Oxford and Canon of Christ Church. See Handbooks of Theology and Leaders of Religion.

Owen (Douglas), Barrister-at-Law, Secretary to the Alliance Marine and General Assurance Company. See Books on Business.

Oxford (M. N.), of Guy's Hospital. A HANDBOOK OF NURSING. *Second Edition. Crown 8vo.* 3s. 6d.

Pakes (W. C. C.). THE SCIENCE OF HYGIENE. With numerous Illustrations. *Demy 8vo.* 15s.

Palmer (Frederick). WITH KUROKI IN MANCHUPIA With many Illustrations. *Second Edition. Demy 8vo. 7s. 6d. net.*
A Colonial Edition is also published.

Parker (Gilbert). A LOVER'S DIARY: SONGS IN SEQUENCE. *Fcap. 8vo.* 5s.

Parkinson (John). PARADISI IN SOLE PARADISUS TERRISTRIS, OR A GARDEN OF ALL SORTS OF PLEASANT FLOWERS. *Folio. £5, 5s. net.*
Also an Edition of 30 copies on Japanese vellum. *Ten Guineas net.*

Parmenter (John). HELIO-TROPES, OR NEW POSIES FOR SUNDIALS, 1625 Edited by PERCIVAL LANDON. *Quarto. 3s. 6d. net.*

Parmentier (Prof. Léon). See Byzantine Texts.

Pascal. See Library of Devotion.

Paston (George). SOCIAL CARICATURES OF THE EIGHTEENTH CENTURY. *Imperial Quarto. £2, 12s. 6d. net.* See also Little Books on Art and Illustrated Pocket Library.

Paterson (W. R.)(Benjamin Swift). LIFE'S QUESTIONINGS. *Crown 8vo. 3s. 6d. net.*

Patterson (A. H.). NOTES OF AN EAST COAST NATURALIST. Illustrated in Colour by F. SOUTHGATE. *Second Edition. Cr. 8vo.* 6s.

Peacock (N.). See Little Books on Art.

Pearce (E. H.), M.A. ANNALS OF CHRIST'S HOSPITAL. With many Illustrations. *Demy 8vo. 7s. 6d.*

Peary (R. E.), Gold Medallist of the Royal Geographical Society. NORTHWARD OVER THE GREAT ICE. With over 800 Illustrations. *2 vols. Royal 8vo. 32s. net.*

Peel (Sidney), late Fellow of Trinity College, Oxford, and Secretary to the Royal Commission on the Licensing Laws. PRACTICAL LICENSING REFORM. *Second Edition. Crown 8vo. 1s. 6d.*

Peters (J. P.), D.D. See Churchman's Library.

Petrie (W. M. Flinders), D.C.L., LL.D., Professor of Egyptology at University College. A HISTORY OF EGYPT, FROM THE EARLIEST TIMES TO THE PRESENT DAY Fully Illustrated. *In six volumes. Crown 8vo. 6s. each.*
VOL. I. PREHISTORIC TIMES TO XVITH DYNASTY. *Fifth Edition.*
VOL. II. THE XVIITH AND XVIIITH DYNASTIES. *Fourth Edition.*
VOL. III. XIXTH TO XXXTH DYNASTIES.
VOL. IV. THE EGYPT OF THE PTOLEMIES. J. P. MAHAFFY, Litt.D.
VOL. V. ROMAN EGYPT. J. G. MILNE, M.A.
VOL. VI. EGYPT IN THE MIDDLE AGES. STANLEY LANE-POOLE, M.A.
RELIGION AND CONSCIENCE IN ANCIENT EGYPT. Fully Illustrated. *Crown 8vo. 2s. 6d.*
SYRIA AND EGYPT, FROM THE TELL EL AMARNA TABLETS. *Crown 8vo. 2s. 6d.*
EGYPTIAN TALES. Illustrated by TRISTRAM ELLIS. *In Two Volumes. Crown 8vo. 3s. 6d. each.*
EGYPTIAN DECORATIVE ART. With 120 Illustrations. *Crown 8vo. 3s. 6d.*

Phillips (W. A.). See Oxford Biographies.

Phillpotts (Eden). MY DEVON YEAR. With 38 Illustrations by J. LEY PETHYBRIDGE. *Second and Cheaper Edition. Large Crown 8vo.* 6s.

Pienaar (Philip). WITH STEYN AND DE WET. *Second Edition. Crown 8vo. 3s. 6d.*

Plautus. THE CAPTIVI. Edited, with an Introduction, Textual Notes, and a Commentary, by W. M. LINDSAY, Fellow of Jesus College, Oxford. *Demy 8vo. 10s. 6d. net.*

Plowden-Wardlaw (J. T.), B.A., King's Coll. Camb. See School Examination Series.

Pocock (Roger). A FRONTIERSMAN. *Third Edition. Crown 8vo.* 6s.
A Colonial Edition is also published.

Podmore (Frank). MODERN SPIRITUALISM. *Two Volumes. Demy 8vo. 21s. net.*
A History and a Criticism.

Poer (J. Patrick Le). A MODERN LEGIONARY. *Crown 8vo.* 6s.
A Colonial Edition is also published.

Pollard (Alice). See Little Books on Art.

Pollard (A. W.). OLD PICTURE BOOKS. With many Illustrations. *Demy 8vo. 7s. 6d. net.*

Pollard (Eliza F.). See Little Books on Art.

Pollock (David), M.I.N.A., Author of 'Modern Shipbuilding and the Men engaged in it, etc., etc. See Books on Business.

Potter (M. C.), M.A., F.L.S. A TEXT-BOOK OF AGRICULTURAL BOTANY. Illustrated. *Second Edition. Crown 8vo. 4s. 6d.*

Potter Boy (An Old). WHEN I WAS A CHILD. *Crown 8vo.* 6s.

Pradeau (G.). A KEY TO THE TIME ALLUSIONS IN THE DIVINE COMEDY. With a Dial. *Small quarto.* 3s. 6d.

Prance (G.). See R. Wyon.

Prescott (O. L.). ABOUT MUSIC, AND WHAT IT IS MADE OF. *Crown 8vo.* 3s. 6d. *net.*

Price (L. L.), M.A., Fellow of Oriel College, Oxon. A HISTORY OF ENGLISH POLITICAL ECONOMY. *Fourth Edition. Crown 8vo.* 2s. 6d.

Primrose (Deborah). A MODERN BŒOTIA. *Crown 8vo.* 6s.

PROTECTION AND INDUSTRY. By various Writers. *Crown 8vo.* 1s. 6d. *net.*

Pugin and Rowlandson. THE MICROCOSM OF LONDON, OR LONDON IN MINIA-TURE. With 104 Illustrations in colour. *In Three Volumes. Small 4to.* £3, 3s. *net.*

'Q' (A. T. Quiller Couch). THE GOLDEN POMP. A Procession of English Lyrics. *Second Edition. Crown 8vo.* 2s. 6d. *net.*

Quevedo Villegas. See Miniature Library.

G.R. and E. S. THE WOODHOUSE CORRESPONDENCE. *Crown 8vo.* 6s.

Rackham (R. B.), M.A. See Westminster Commentaries.

Randolph (B. W.), D.D., Principal of the Theological College, Ely. See Library of Devotion.

Rannie (D. W.), M.A. A STUDENT'S HISTORY OF SCOTLAND. *Cr. 8vo.* 3s. 6d.

Rashdall (Hastings), M.A., Fellow and Tutor of New College, Oxford. DOCTRINE AND DEVELOPMENT. *Crown 8vo.* 6s.

Rawstorne (Lawrence, Esq.). See Illustrated Pocket Library.

A Real Paddy. See Illustrated Pocket Library.

Reason (W.), M.A. See Social Questions Series.

Redfern (W. B.), Author of 'Ancient Wood and Iron Work in Cambridge,' etc. ROYAL AND HISTORIC GLOVES AND ANCIENT SHOES. Profusely Illustrated in colour and half-tone. *Quarto,* £2, 2s. *net.*

Reynolds. See Little Galleries.

Roberts (M. E.). See C. C. Channer.

Robertson, (A.), D.D., Lord Bishop of Exeter. REGNUM DEI. The Bampton Lectures of 1901. *Demy 8vo.* 12s. 6d. *net.*

Robertson (C. Grant), M.A., Fellow of All Souls' College, Oxford, Examiner in the Honour School of Modern History, Oxford, 1901-1904. SELECT STATUTES, CASES, AND CONSTITUTIONAL DOCUMENTS, 1660-1832. *Demy 8vo.* 10s. 6d. *net.*

*Robertson (Sir G. S.) K.C.S.I. CHITRAL: The Story of a Minor Siege. With numerous Illustrations, Map and Plans. *Fourth Edition. Crown 8vo.* 2s. 6d. *net.*

Robinson (A. W.), M.A. See Churchman's Bible.

Robinson (Cecilia), THE MINISTRY OF DEACONESSES. With an Introduction by the late Archbishop of Canterbury. *Crown 8vo.* 3s. 6d.

Rochefoucauld (La), See Little Library.

Rodwell (G.), B.A. NEW TESTAMENT GREEK. A Course for Beginners. With a Preface by WALTER LOCK, D.D., Warden of Keble College. *Fcap. 8vo.* 3s. 6d.

Roe (Fred). ANCIENT COFFERS AND CUPBOARDS: Their History and Description. With many Illustrations. *Quarto.* £3, 3s. *net.*

Rogers (A. G. L.), M.A., Editor of the last volume of 'The History of Agriculture and Prices in Engand.' See Books on Business.

Romney. See Little Galleries.

Roscoe (E. S.). ROBERT HARLEY, EARL OF OXFORD. Illustrated. *Demy 8vo.* 7s. 6d. This is the only life of Harley in existence.
See also The Little Guides.

Rose (Edward). THE ROSE READER. With numerous Illustrations. *Crown 8vo.* 2s. 6d. Also in 4 Parts. Parts I. and II. 6d. each; Part III. 8d.; Part IV. 10d.

Rubie (A. E.), D.D., Head Master of College, Eltham. See Junior School Books.

Russell (W. Clark). THE LIFE OF ADMIRAL LORD COLLINGWOOD. With Illustrations by F. BRANGWYN. *Fourth Edition. Crown 8vo.* 6s.
A Colonial Edition is also published.

St. Anselm. See Library of Devotion.

St. Augustine. See Library of Devotion.

'Saki' (H. Munro). REGINALD. *Second Edition. Fcap. 8vo.* 2s. 6d. *net.*

Sales (St. Francis de). See Library of Devotion.

Salmon (A. L.). A POPULAR GUIDE TO DEVON. *Medium 8vo.* 6d. *net.* See also The Little Guides.

Sargeaunt (J.), M.A. ANNALS OF WESTMINSTER SCHOOL. With numerous Illustrations. *Demy 8vo.* 7s. 6d.

Sathas (C.), See Byzantine Texts.

Schmitt (John). See Byzantine Texts.
Scott, (A. M.) WINSTON SPENCER CHURCHILL. With Portraits and Illustrations. *Crown 8vo.* 3s. 6d.
Seeley (H. G.) F.R.S. DRAGONS OF THE AIR. With many Illustrations. *Cr. 8vo.* 6s.
*Selincourt (E. de), M.A. THE POEMS OF JOHN KEATS. With an Introduction and Notes, and a Portrait in Photogravure. *Demy 8vo.* 7s. 6d. net.
Sells (V. P.), M.A. THE MECHANICS OF DAILY LIFE. Illustrated. *Cr. 8vo.* 2s. 6d.
Selous (Edmund). TOMMY SMITH'S ANIMALS. Illustrated by G. W. ORD. *Third Edition. Fcap. 8vo.* 2s. 6d.
Settle (J. H.). ANECDOTES OF SOLDIERS. *Crown 8vo.* 3s. 6d. net.
  A Colonial Edition is also published.
Shakespeare (William).
THE FOUR FOLIOS, 1623; 1632; 1664; 1685. Each *Four Guineas net*, or a complete set, *Twelve Guineas net.*
The Arden Shakespeare.
  Demy 8vo. 2s. 6d. net each volume. General Editor, W. J. CRAIG. An Edition of Shakespeare in single Plays. Edited with a full Introduction, Textual Notes, and a Commentary at the foot of the page.
HAMLET. Edited by EDWARD DOWDEN, Litt.D.
ROMEO AND JULIET. Edited by EDWARD DOWDEN, Litt.D.
KING LEAR. Edited by W. J. CRAIG.
JULIUS CAESAR. Edited by M. MACMILLAN, M.A.
THE TEMPEST. Edited by MORETON LUCE.
OTHELLO. Edited by H. C. HART.
TITUS ANDRONICUS. Edited by H. B. BAILDON.
CYMBELINE. Edited by EDWARD DOWDEN.
THE MERRY WIVES OF WINDSOR. Edited by H. C. HART.
A MIDSUMMER NIGHT'S DREAM. Edited by H. CUNINGHAM.
KING HENRY V. Edited by H. A. EVANS.
ALL'S WELL THAT ENDS WELL. Edited by W. O. BRIGSTOCKE.
THE TAMING OF THE SHREW. Edited by R. WARWICK BOND.
TIMON OF ATHENS. Edited by K. DEIGHTON.
The Little Quarto Shakespeare. Edited by W. J. CRAIG. With Introductions and Notes.
  Pott 16mo. In 40 Volumes. Leather, price 1s. net each volume.
  See also Methuen's Universal Library.
Sharp (A.). VICTORIAN POETS. *Crown 8vo.* 2s. 6d.
Sharp (Mrs. E. A.). See Little Books on Art.
Shedlock (J. S.). THE PIANOFORTE SONATA: Its Origin and Development. *Crown 8vo.* 5s.
Shelley (Percy B.). ADONAIS; an Elegy on the death of John Keats, Author of 'Endymion,' etc. Pisa. From the types of Didot, 1821. 2s. net.
  See also Methuen's Universal Library.
Sherwell (Arthur), M.A. See Social Questions Series.
*Shipley (Mary E.). AN ENGLISH CHURCH HISTORY FOR CHILDREN. With a Preface by the Bishop of Gibraltar, late Professor of Ecclesiastical History at King's College, London. With Maps and Illustrations. Part I. *Crown 8vo.* 2s. 6d. net.
Sichel (Walter). DISRAELI: A Study in Personality and Ideas. With 3 Portraits. *Demy 8vo.* 12s. 6d. net.
  A Colonial Edition is also published.
  See also Oxford Biographies.
Sime (J.). See Little Books on Art.
Simonson (G. A.). FRANCESCO GUARDI. With 41 Plates. *Royal folio.* £2, 2s. net.
Sketchley (R. E. D.). See Little Books on Art.
Skipton (H. P. K.). See Little Books on Art.
Sladen (Douglas). SICILY. With over 200 Illustrations. *Crown 8vo.* 5s. net.
Small (Evan), M.A. THE EARTH. An Introduction to Physiography. Illustrated. *Crown 8vo.* 2s. 6d.
Smallwood, (M. G.). See Little Books on Art.
Smedley (F. E.). See Illustrated Pocket Library.
Smith (Adam). THE WEALTH OF NATIONS. Edited with an Introduction and numerous Notes by EDWIN CANNAN, M.A. *Two volumes. Demy 8vo.* 21s. net.
  See also Methuen's Universal Library.
Smith (Horace and James). See Little Library.
Snell (F. J.). A BOOK OF EXMOOR. Illustrated. *Crown 8vo.* 6s.
Sophocles. See Classical Translations.

Sornet (L. A.), Modern Language Master at King Edward School, Birmingham. See Junior School Books.

South (Wilton E.), M.A. See Junior School Books.

Southey (R.) ENGLISH SEAMEN. Edited, with an Introduction, by DAVID HANNAY. Vol. I. (Howard, Clifford, Hawkins, Drake, Cavendish). *Second Edition. Crown 8vo. 6s.* Vol. II. (Richard Hawkins, Grenville, Essex, and Raleigh). *Crown 8vo. 6s.*

Spence (C. H.), M.A., Clifton College. See School Examination Series.

Spooner (W. A.), M.A., Warden of New College, Oxford. See Leaders of Religion.

Stanbridge (J. W.), B.D., late Canon of York, and sometime Fellow of St. John's College, Oxford. See Library of Devotion.

'Stancliffe.' GOLF DO'S AND DONT'S. *Second Edition. Fcap. 8vo. 1s.*

Stedman (A. M. M.), M.A.

INITIA LATINA : Easy Lessons on Elementary Accidence. *Seventh Edition. Fcap. 8vo. 1s.*

FIRST LATIN LESSONS. *Eighth Edition. Crown 8vo. 2s.*

FIRST LATIN READER. With Notes adapted to the Shorter Latin Primer and Vocabulary. *Sixth Edition revised. 18mo. 1s. 6d.*

EASY SELECTIONS FROM CÆSAR. The Helvetian War. *Second Edition. 18mo. 1s.*

EASY SELECTIONS FROM LIVY. Part I. The Kings of Rome. *18mo. Second Edition. 1s. 6d.*

EASY LATIN PASSAGES FOR UNSEEN TRANSLATION. *Tenth Edition. Fcap. 8vo. 1s. 6d.*

EXEMPLA LATINA. First Exercises in Latin Accidence. With Vocabulary. *Third Edition. Crown 8vo. 1s.*

EASY LATIN EXERCISES ON THE SYNTAX OF THE SHORTER AND REVISED LATIN PRIMER. With Vocabulary. *Ninth and Cheaper Edition, rewritten. Crown 8vo. 1s. 6d. Original Edition. 2s. 6d.* KEY, 3s. net.

THE LATIN COMPOUND SENTENCE : Rules and Exercises. *Second Edition. Crown 8vo. 1s. 6d.* With Vocabulary. 2s.

NOTANDA QUAEDAM : Miscellaneous Latin Exercises on Common Rules and Idioms. *Fourth Edition. Fcap. 8vo. 1s. 6d.* With Vocabulary. 2s. Key, 2s. net.

LATIN VOCABULARIES FOR REPETITION : Arranged according to Subjects. *Twelfth Edition. Fcap. 8vo. 1s. 6d.*

A VOCABULARY OF LATIN IDIOMS. *18mo. Second Edition. 1s.*

STEPS TO GREEK. *Second Edition, revised. 18mo. 1s.*

A SHORTER GREEK PRIMER. *Crown 8vo. 1s. 6d.*

EASY GREEK PASSAGES FOR UNSEEN TRANSLATION. *Third Edition, revised. Fcap. 8vo. 1s. 6d.*

GREEK VOCABULARIES FOR REPETITION. Arranged according to Subjects. *Third Edition. Fcap. 8vo. 1s. 6d.*

GREEK TESTAMENT SELECTIONS. For the use of Schools. With Introduction, Notes, and Vocabulary. *Third Edition. Fcap. 8vo. 2s. 6d.*

STEPS TO FRENCH. *Sixth Edition. 18mo. 8d.*

FIRST FRENCH LESSONS. *Sixth Edition, revised. Crown 8vo. 1s.*

EASY FRENCH PASSAGES FOR UNSEEN TRANSLATION. *Fifth Edition. revised. Fcap. 8vo. 1s. 6d.*

EASY FRENCH EXERCISES ON ELEMENTARY SYNTAX. With Vocabulary. *Fourth Edition. Crown 8vo. 2s. 6d.* KEY. 3s. net.

FRENCH VOCABULARIES FOR REPETITION : Arranged according to Subjects. *Twelfth Edition. Fcap. 8vo. 1s.*

Steel (R. Elliott), M.A., F.C.S. THE WORLD OF SCIENCE. Including Chemistry, Heat, Light, Sound, Magnetism, Electricity, Botany, Zoology, Physiology, Astronomy, and Geology. 147 Illustrations. *Second Edition. Crown 8vo. 2s. 6d.* See also School Examination Series.

Stephenson (C.), of the Technical College, Bradford, and **Suddards (F.)** of the Yorkshire College, Leeds. ORNAMENTAL DESIGN FOR WOVEN FABRICS. Illustrated. *Demy 8vo. Second Edition. 7s. 6d.*

Stephenson (J.), M.A. THE CHIEF TRUTHS OF THE CHRISTIAN FAITH *Crown 8vo. 3s. 6d.*

Sterne (Laurence). See Little Library.

Sterry (W.), M.A. ANNALS OF ETON COLLEGE. With numerous Illustrations. *Demy 8vo. 7s. 6d.*

Steuart (Katherine), BY ALLAN WATER. *Second Edition. Crown 8vo. 6s.*

Stevenson (R. L.). THE LETTERS OF ROBERT LOUIS STEVENSON TO HIS FAMILY AND FRIENDS. Selected and Edited, with Notes and Introductions, by SIDNEY COLVIN. *Sixth and Cheaper Edition. Crown 8vo. 12s.*

A 3

LIBRARY EDITION. *Demy 8vo. 2 vols. 25s. net.*
    A Colonial Edition is also published.
VAILIMA LETTERS. With an Etched Portrait by WILLIAM STRANG. *Fourth Edition. Crown 8vo. Buckram. 6s.*
    A Colonial Edition is also published.
THE LIFE OF R. L. STEVENSON. See G. Balfour.
Stevenson (M. I.). FROM SARANAC TO THE MARQUESAS. Being Letters written by Mrs. M. I. STEVENSON during 1887-8 to her sister, Miss JANE WHYTE BALFOUR. With an Introduction by GEORGE W. BALFOUR, M.D., LL.D., F.R.S.S. *Crown 8vo. 6s. net.*
    A Colonial Edition is also published.
Stoddart (Anna M.). See Oxford Biographies.
Stone (E. D.), M.A., late Assistant Master at Eton. SELECTIONS FROM THE ODYSSEY. *Fcap. 8vo. 1s. 6d.*
Stone (S. J.). POEMS AND HYMNS. With a Memoir by F. G. ELLERTON, M.A. With Portrait. *Crown 8vo. 6s.*
Straker (F.), Assoc. of the Institute of Bankers, and Lecturer to the London Chamber of Commerce. See Books on Business.
Streane (A. W.), D.D. See Churchman's Bible.
Stroud (H.), D.Sc., M.A., Professor of Physics in the Durham College of Science, Newcastle-on-Tyne. See Textbooks of Technology.
Strutt (Joseph). THE SPORTS AND PASTIMES OF THE PEOPLE OF ENGLAND. Illustrated by many engravings. Revised by J. CHARLES COX, LL.D., F.S.A. *Quarto. 21s. net.*
Stuart (Capt. Donald). THE STRUGGLE FOR PERSIA. With a Map. *Crown 8vo. 6s.*
Sturch (F.), Manual Training Instructor to the Surrey County Council. SOLUTIONS TO THE CITY AND GUILDS QUESTIONS IN MANUAL INSTRUCTION DRAW-ING. *Imp. 4to. 2s.*
Suckling (Sir John). FRAGMENTA AUREA: a Collection of all the Incomparable Peeces, written by. And published by a friend to perpetuate his memory. Printed by his own copies.
    Printed for HUMPHREY MOSELEY, and are to be sold at his shop, at the sign of the Princes Arms in St. Paul's Churchyard, 1646.
Suddards (F.). See C. Stephenson.
Surtees (R. S.). See Illustrated Pocket Library.
Swift (Jonathan). THE JOURNAL TO STELLA. Edited by G. A. AITKEN. *Cr. 8vo. 6s.*
Symes (J. E.), M.A. THE FRENCH REVOLUTION. *Second Edition. Crown 8vo. 2s. 6d.*
Syrett (Netta). See Little Blue Books.
Tacitus. AGRICOLA. With Introduction, Notes, Map, etc. By R. F. DAVIS, M.A., late Assistant Master at Weymouth College. *Fcap. 8vo. 2s.*
GERMANIA. By the same Editor. *Fcap. 8vo. 2s.* See also Classical Translations.
Tauler (J.). See Library of Devotion.
Taunton (E. L.). A HISTORY OF THE JESUITS IN ENGLAND. With Illustrations. *Demy 8vo. 21s. net.*
Taylor (A. E.). THE ELEMENTS OF METAPHYSICS. *Demy 8vo. 10s. 6d. net.*
Taylor (F. G.), M.A. See Commercial Series.
Taylor (I. A.). See Oxford Biographies.
Taylor (T. M.), M.A., Fellow of Gonville and Caius College, Cambridge. A CONSTI-TUTIONAL AND POLITICAL HISTORY OF ROME. *Crown 8vo. 7s. 6d.*
Tennyson (Alfred, Lord). THE EARLY POEMS OF. Edted, with Notes and an Introduction, by J. CHURTON COLLINS, M.A. *Crown 8vo. 6s.* i
IN MEMORIAM, MAUD, AND THE PRINCESS. Edited by J. CHURTON COLLINS, M.A. *Crown 8vo. 6s.* See also Little Library.
Terry (C. S.). See Oxford Biographies.
Terton (Alice). LIGHTS AND SHADOWS IN A HOSPITAL. *Crown 8vo. 3s. 6d.*
Thackeray (W. M.). See Little Library.
Theobald (F. W.), M.A. INSECT LIFE. Illustrated. *Second Ed. Revised. Cr. 8vo. 2s. 6d.*
Thompson (A. H.). See The Little Guides.
Tileston (Mary W.). DAILY STRENGTH FOR DAILY NEEDS. *Tenth Edition. Fcap. 8vo. 2s. 6d. net.* Also editions in superior binding 5s. and 6s.
Tompkins (H. W.), F.R.H.S. See The Little Guides.
Townley (Lady Susan). MY CHINESE NOTE-BOOK With 16 Illustrations and 2 Maps. *Third Edition. Demy 8vo. 10s. 6d. net.*
    A Colonial Edition is also published.
Toynbee (Paget), M.A., D.Litt. DANTE STUDIES AND RESEARCHES. *Demy 8vo. 10s. 6d. net.* See also Oxford Biographies.

Trench (Herbert). DEIRDRE WED: and Other Poems. *Crown 8vo.* 5*s.*
Trevelyan (G. M.) Fellow of Trinity College, Cambridge. ENGLAND UNDER THE STUARTS. With Maps and Plans. *Demy 8vo.* 10*s. 6d. net.*
Troutbeck (G. E.). See The Little Guides.
Tuckwell (Gertrude). See Social Questions Series.
Twining (Louisa). See Social Questions Series.
Tyler (E. A.), B.A., F.C.S., Head of Chemical Department, Swansea Technical College. See Junior School Books.
Tyrell-Gill (Frances). See Little Books on Art.
Vaughan (Henry). See Little Library.
Voegelin (A.), M.A. See Junior Examination Series.
Wade (G. W.), D.D. OLD TESTAMENT HISTORY. With Maps. *Third Edition. Crown 8vo.* 6*s.*
Wagner (Richard). See A. L. Cleather.
Wall (J. C.) DEVILS. Illustrated by the Author and from photographs. *Demy 8vo.* 4*s. 6d. net.* See also The Antiquary's Books.
Walters (H. B.). See Little Books on Art.
Walton (Isaac) and **Cotton (Charles).** See Illustrated Pocket Library, Methuen's Universal Library, and Little Library.
Warmelo (D. S. Van). ON COMMANDO. With Portrait. *Crown 8vo.* 3*s. 6d.*
Waterhouse (Mrs. Alfred). WITH THE SIMPLE-HEARTED: Little Homilies to Women in Country Places. *Small Pott 8vo.* 2*s. net.* See also Little Library.
Weatherhead (T. C.), M.A. EXAMINATION PAPERS IN HORACE. *Crown 8vo.* 2*s.* See also Junior Examination Series.
Webb (W. T.). See Little Blue Books.
Webber (F. C.). See Textbooks of Technology.
Wells (Sidney H.). See Textbooks of Technology.
Wells (J.), M.A., Fellow and Tutor of Wadham College. OXFORD AND OXFORD LIFE. By Members of the University. *Third Edition Crown 8vo.* 3*s. 6d.*
A SHORT HISTORY OF ROME. *Fifth Edition.* With 3 Maps. *Cr. 8vo.* 3*s. 6d.*
This book is intended for the Middle and Upper Forms of Public Schools and for Pass Students at the Universities. It contains copious Tables, etc. See also The Little Guides.
Wetmore (Helen C.). THE LAST OF THE GREAT SCOUTS ('Buffalo Bill'). With Illustrations. *Second Edition. Demy 8vo.* 6*s.*
Whibley (C.). See Henley and Whibley.
Whibley (L.), M.A., Fellow of Pembroke College, Cambridge. GREEK OLIGARCHIES: THEIR ORGANISATION AND CHARACTER. *Crown 8vo.* 6*s.*
Whitaker (G. H.), M.A. See Churchman's Bible.
White (Gilbert). THE NATURAL HISTORY OF SELBORNE. Edited by L. C. MIALL, F.R.S., assisted by W. WARDE FOWLER, M.A. *Crown 8vo.* 6*s.* See also Methuen's Universal Library.
Whitfield (E. E.). See Commercial Series.
Whitehead (A. W.). GASPARD DE COLIGNY. With many Illustrations. *Demy 8vo.* 12*s. 6d. net.*
Whitley (Miss). See Social Questions Series.
Whyte (A. G.), B.Sc., Editor of *Electrical Investments.* See Books on Business.
Wilberforce (Wilfrid) See Little Books on Art.
Wilde (Oscar). DE PROFUNDIS. *Crown 8vo.* 5*s. net.*
Also a Limited Edition on Japanese Vellum. *Demy 8vo.* £2, 2*s. net*; and a Limited Edition on hand-made paper. *Demy 8vo.* 21*s. net.* A Colonial Edition is also published.
Wilkins (W. H.), B.A. See Social Questions Series.
Wilkinson (J. Frome). See Social Questions Series.
Williamson (W.). THE BRITISH GARDENER. Illustrated. *Demy 8vo.* 10*s. 6d.*
Williamson (W.), B.A. EASY DICTATION AND SPELLING. *Third Edition. Fcap. 8vo.* 1*s.* See also Junior Examination Series and Junior School Books.
Wilmot-Buxton (E. M.). MAKERS OF EUROPE. *Crown 8vo. Third Edition.* 3*s. 6d.*
A Text-book of European History for Middle Forms.
THE ANCIENT WORLD. With Maps and Illustrations. *Crown 8vo.* 3*s. 6d.*
See also The Beginner's Books.
Wilson (Bishop). See Library of Devotion.
Willson (Beckles). LORD STRATHCONA: the Story of his Life. Illustrated. *Demy 8vo.* 7*s. 6d.*
A Colonial Edition is also published.
Wilson (A. J.), Editor of the *Investor's Review*, City Editor of the *Daily Chronicle.* See Books on Business.
Wilson (H. A.). See Books on Business.

Wilton (Richard), M.A.   LYRA PASTORALIS : Songs of Nature, Church, and Home. *Pott 8vo. 2s. 6d.*
A volume of devotional poems.

Winbolt (S. E.), M.A., Assistant Master in Christ's Hospital.   EXERCISES IN LATIN ACCIDENCE.   *Crown 8vo.   1s. 6d.*
An elementary book adapted for Lower Forms to accompany the Shorter Latin Primer.
LATIN HEXAMETER VERSE : An Aid to Composition. *Crown 8vo.   3s. 6d.* KEY, 5s. net.

Windle (B. C. A.), D.Sc., F.R.S.   See Antiquary's Books and The Little Guides.

Winterbotham (Canon), M.A., B.Sc., LL.B.   See Churchman's Library.

Wood (J. A. E.).   See Textbooks of Technology.

Wordsworth (Christopher).   See Antiquary's Books.

Wordsworth (W.).   See Little Library.

Wordsworth (W.) and Coleridge (S. T.).   See Little Library.

Wright (Arthur), M.A., Fellow of Queen's College, Cambridge.   See Churchman's Library.

Wright (Sophie). GERMAN VOCABULARIES FOR REPETITION. *Fcap. 8vo.   1s. 6d.*

*Wrong, (George M.), Professor of History in the University of Toronto.   THE EARL OF ELGIN.   With Illustrations. *Demy 8vo.   7s. 6d. net.*

Wylde (A. B.).   MODERN ABYSSINIA.   With a Map and a Portrait.   *Demy 8vo. 15s. net.*

Wyndham (G.), M.P.   THE POEMS OF WILLIAM SHAKESPEARE.   With an Introduction and Notes. *Demy 8vo. Buckram, gilt top. 10s. 6d.*

Wyon (R.) and France (G.).   THE LAND OF THE BLACK MOUNTAIN.   Being a description of Montenegro. With 40 Illustrations. *Crown 8vo.   6s.*
A Colonial Edition is also published.

Yeats (W. B.).   AN ANTHOLOGY OF IRISH VERSE.   *Revised and Enlarged Edition.   Crown 8vo.   3s. 6d.*

Yendis (M.). THE GREAT RED FROG.   A Story told in 40 Coloured Pictures. *Fcap. 8vo.   1s. net.*

Young (Filson).   THE COMPLETE MOTORIST.   With 138 Illustrations.   *Third Edition. Demy 8vo.   12s. 6d. net.*

Young (T. M.).   THE AMERICAN COTTON INDUSTRY : A Study of Work and Workers.   With an Introduction by ELIJAH HELM, Secretary to the Manchester Chamber of Commerce. *Crown 8vo.   Cloth, 2s. 6d. ; paper boards, 1s. 6d.*

Zenker (E. V.).   ANARCHISM.   *Demy 8vo.   7s. 6d.*

Zimmern (Antonia).   WHAT DO WE KNOW CONCERNING ELECTRICITY?   *Crown 8vo.   1s. 6d. net.*

Antiquary's Books, The

General Editor, J. CHARLES COX, LL.D., F.S.A.

A series of volumes dealing with various branches of English Antiquities ; comprehensive and popular, as well as accurate and scholarly.

ENGLISH MONASTIC LIFE.   By the Right Rev. Abbot Gasquet, O.S.B.   Illustrated. *Second Edition, revised. Demy 8vo.   7s. 6d. net.*

REMAINS OF THE PREHISTORIC AGE IN ENGLAND.   By B. C. A. Windle, D.Sc., F.R.S. With numerous Illustrations and Plans. *Demy 8vo.   7s. 6d. net.*

OLD SERVICE BOOKS OF THE ENGLISH CHURCH.   By Christopher Wordsworth, M.A., and Henry Littlehales. With Coloured and other Illustrations. *Demy 8vo.   7s. 6d. net.*

CELTIC ART.   By J. Romilly Allen, F.S.A. With numerous Illustrations and Plans. *Demy 8vo.   7s. 6d. net.*

*ARCHÆOLOGY AND FALSE ANTIQUITIES.   By R. Munro, LL.D.   With numerous Illustrations. *Demy 8vo.   7s. 6d. net.*

SHRINES OF BRITISH SAINTS.   By J. C. WALL.   With numerous Illustrations and Plans. *Demy 8vo.   7s. 6d. net.*

Beginner's Books, The

*EASY FRENCH RHYMES.   By Henri Blouet.   Illustrated. *Fcap. 8vo.   1s.*

*EASY STORIES FROM ENGLISH HISTORY.   By E. M. Wilmot-Buxton, Author of ' Makers of Europe.' *Fcap. 8vo.   1s.*

Business, Books on

Crown 8vo.   2s. 6d. net.

A series of volumes dealing with all the most important aspects of commercial and financial activity.   The volumes are intended to treat separately all the considerable

Industries and forms of business, and to explain accurately and clearly what they do and how they do it. The first Twelve volumes are—

PORTS AND DOCKS. By Douglas Owen.
RAILWAYS. By E. R. McDermott.
THE STOCK EXCHANGE. By Chas. Duguid. *Second Edition.*
THE BUSINESS OF INSURANCE. By A. J. Wilson.
THE ELECTRICAL INDUSTRY: LIGHTING, TRACTION, AND POWER. By A. G. Whyte, B.Sc.
THE SHIPBUILDING INDUSTRY. By David Pollock, M.I.N.A.
THE MONEY MARKET. By F. Straker.
THE BUSINESS SIDE OF AGRICULTURE. By A. G. L. Rogers, M.A.
LAW IN BUSINESS. By H. A. Wilson.
THE BREWING INDUSTRY. By Julian L. Baker, F.I.C., F.C.S.
THE AUTOMOBILE INDUSTRY. By G. de H. Stone.
MINING AND MINING INVESTMENTS. By 'A. Moil.'
*THE BUSINESS OF ADVERTISING. By Clarence G. Moran, Barrister-at-Law. Illustrated.
*TRADE UNIONS. By G. Drage.
*CIVIL ENGINEERING. By T. Claxton Fidler, M.Inst. C.E. Illustrated.
*THE COAL INDUSTRY. By Ernest Aves. Illustrated.

Byzantine Texts

Edited by J. B. BURY, M.A., Litt.D.

A series of texts of Byzantine Historians, edited by English and foreign scholars.
ZACHARIAH OF MITYLENE. Translated by F. J. Hamilton, D.D., and E. W. Brooks. *Demy 8vo.* 12s. 6d. *net.*
EVAGRIUS. Edited by Léon Parmentier and M. Bidez. *Demy 8vo.* 10s. 6d. *net.*
THE HISTORY OF PSELLUS. Edited by C. Sathas. *Demy 8vo.* 15s. *net.*
ECTHESIS CHRONICA. Edited by Professor Lambros. *Demy 8vo.* 7s. 6d. *net.*
THE CHRONICLE OF MOREA. Edited by John Schmitt. *Demy 8vo.* 15s. *net.*

Churchman's Bible, The

General Editor, J. H. BURN, B.D., F.R.S.E.

A series of Expositions on the Books of the Bible, which will be of service to the general reader in the practical and devotional study of the Sacred Text.

Each Book is provided with a full and clear Introductory Section, in which is stated what is known or conjectured respecting the date and occasion of the composition of the Book, and any other particulars that may help to elucidate its meaning as a whole. The Exposition is divided into sections of a convenient length, corresponding as far as possible with the divisions of the Church Lectionary. The Translation of the Authorised Version is printed in full, such corrections as are deemed necessary being placed in footnotes.

THE EPISTLE TO THE GALATIANS. Edited by A. W. Robinson, M.A. *Second Edition. Fcap. 8vo.* 1s. 6d. *net.*
ECCLESIASTES. Edited by A. W. Streane, D.D. *Fcap. 8vo.* 1s. 6d. *net.*
THE EPISTLE TO THE PHILIPPIANS. Edited by C. R. D. Biggs, D.D. *Fcap 8vo.* 1s. 6d. *net.*
THE EPISTLE OF ST. JAMES. Edited by H. W. Fulford, M.A. *Fcap. 8vo.* 1s. 6d. *net.*
ISAIAH. Edited by W. E. Barnes, D.D. *Two Volumes. Fcap. 8vo.* 2s. *net each.* With Map.
THE EPISTLE OF ST. PAUL THE APOSTLE TO THE EPHESIANS. Edited by G. H. Whitaker, M.A. *Fcap. 8vo.* 1s. 6d. *net.*

Churchman's Library, The

General Editor, J. H. BURN, B.D., F.R.S.E.,

A series of volumes upon such questions as are occupying the attention of Church people at the present time. The Editor has enlisted the services of a band of scholars, who, having made a special study of their respective subjects, are in a position to furnish the best results of modern research accurately and attractively.

THE BEGINNINGS OF ENGLISH CHRISTIANITY. By W. E. Collins, M.A. With Map. *Crown 8vo.* 3s. 6d.
SOME NEW TESTAMENT PROBLEMS. By Arthur Wright, M.A. *Crown 8vo.* 6s.

THE KINGDOM OF HEAVEN HERE AND HEREAFTER. By Canon Winterbotham, M.A., B.Sc.;
LL.B. *Crown 8vo.* 3*s.* 6*d.*
THE WORKMANSHIP OF THE PRAYER BOOK: Its Literary and Liturgical Aspects. By
J. Dowden, D.D. *Second Edition. Crown 8vo.* 3*s.* 6*d.*
EVOLUTION. By F. B. Jevons, M.A., Litt.D. *Crown 8vo.* 3*s.* 6*d.*
THE OLD TESTAMENT AND THE NEW SCHOLARSHIP. By J. W. Peters, D.D. *Crown 8vo.* 6*s.*
THE CHURCHMAN'S INTRODUCTION TO THE OLD TESTAMENT. By A. M. Mackay, B.A.
Crown 8vo. 3*s.* 6*d.*
THE CHURCH OF CHRIST. By E. T. Green, M.A. *Crown 8vo.* 6*s.*
COMPARATIVE THEOLOGY. By J. A. MacCulloch. *Crown 8vo.* 6*s.*

Classical Translations

Edited by H. F. Fox, M.A., Fellow and Tutor of Brasenose College, Oxford.

Crown 8vo.

A series of Translations from the Greek and Latin Classics. The Publishers have
enlisted the services of some of the best Oxford and Cambridge Scholars, and it is
their intention that the series shall be distinguished by literary excellence as well as
by scholarly accuracy.

ÆSCHYLUS—Agamemnon, Choephoroe, Eumenides. Translated by Lewis Campbell, LL.D. 5*s.*
CICERO—De Oratore I. Translated by E. N. P. Moor, M.A. 3*s.* 6*d.*
CICERO—Select Orations (Pro Milone, Pro Mureno, Philippic II., in Catilinam). Translated
by H. E. D. BLAKISTON, M.A. 5*s.*
CICERO—De Natura Deorum. Translated by F. Brooks, M.A. 3*s.* 6*d.*
CICERO—De Officiis. Translated by G. B. Gardiner, M.A. 2*s.* 6*d.*
HORACE—The Odes and Epodes. Translated by A. D. Godley, M.A. 2*s.*
LUCIAN—Six Dialogues (Nigrinus, Icaro-Menippus, The Cock, The Ship, The Parasite, The
Lover of Falsehood). Translated by S. T. Irwin, M.A. 3*s.* 6*d.*
SOPHOCLES—Electra and Ajax. Translated by E. D. A. Morshead, M.A. 2*s.* 6*d.*
TACITUS—Agricola and Germania. Translated by R. B. Townshend. 2*s.* 6*d.*
THE SATIRES OF JUVENAL. Translated by S. G. Owen. 2*s.* 6*d.*

Commercial Series, Methuen's

Edited by H. DE B. GIBBINS, Litt. D., M.A.

Crown 8vo.

A series intended to assist students and young men preparing for a commercial
career, by supplying useful handbooks of a clear and practical character, dealing
with those subjects which are absolutely essential in the business life.

COMMERCIAL EDUCATION IN THEORY AND PRACTICE. By E. E. Whitfield, M.A. 5*s.*
An introduction to Methuen's Commercial Series treating the question of Commercial
Education fully from both the point of view of the teacher and of the parent.
BRITISH COMMERCE AND COLONIES FROM ELIZABETH TO VICTORIA. By H. de B. Gibbins,
Litt.D., M.A. *Third Edition.* 2*s.*
COMMERCIAL EXAMINATION PAPERS. By H. de B. Gibbins, Litt.D., M.A. 1*s.* 6*d.*
THE ECONOMICS OF COMMERCE, By H. de B. Gibbins, Litt.D., M.A. 1*s.* 6*d.*
A GERMAN COMMERCIAL READER. By S. E. Bally. With Vocabulary. 2*s.*
A COMMERCIAL GEOGRAPHY OF THE BRITISH EMPIRE. By L. W. Lyde, M.A. *Fourth
Edition.* 2*s.*
A COMMERCIAL GEOGRAPHY OF FOREIGN NATIONS. By F. C. Boon, B.A. 2*s.*
A PRIMER OF BUSINESS. By S. Jackson, M.A. *Third Edition.* 1*s.* 6*d.*
COMMERCIAL ARITHMETIC. By F. G. Taylor, M.A. *Third Edition.* 1*s.* 6*d.*
FRENCH COMMERCIAL CORRESPONDENCE. By S. E. Bally. With Vocabulary. *Third
Edition.* 2*s.*
GERMAN COMMERCIAL CORRESPONDENCE. By S. E. Bally. with Vocabulary. 2*s.* 6*d.*
A FRENCH COMMERCIAL READER. By S. E. Bally. With Vocabulary. *Second Edition.* 2*s.*
PRECIS WRITING AND OFFICE CORRESPONDENCE. By E. E. Whitfield, M.A. *Second
Edition.* 2*s.*
A GUIDE TO PROFESSIONS AND BUSINESS. By H. Jones. 1*s.* 6*d.*
THE PRINCIPLES OF BOOK-KEEPING BY DOUBLE ENTRY. By J. E. B. M'Allen, M.A. 2*s.*
COMMERCIAL LAW. By W. Douglas Edwards. 2*s.*

Connoisseur's Library, The

Wide Royal 8vo. 25s. net.

A sumptuous series of 20 books on art, written by experts for collectors, superbly illustrated in photogravure, collotype, and colour. The technical side of the art is duly treated. The first volumes are—

MEZZOTINTS. By Cyril Davenport. With 40 Plates in Photogravure.

PORCELAIN. By Edward Dillon. With 19 Plates in Colour, 20 in Collotype, and 5 in Photogravure.

*MINIATURES. By Dudley Heath. With 9 Plates in Colour, 15 in Collotype, and 15 in Photogravure.

*IVORIES. By A. Maskell. With 80 Plates in Collotype and Photogravure.

Devotion, The Library of

With Introductions and (where necessary) Notes.

Small Pott 8vo, cloth, 2s. ; leather, 2s. 6d. net.

The masterpieces of devotional literature. The books are furnished with such Introductions and Notes as may be necessary to explain the standpoint of the author and the obvious difficulties of the text, without unnecessary intrusion between the author and the devout mind.

THE CONFESSIONS OF ST. AUGUSTINE. Edited by C. Bigg, D.D. *Third Edition.*
THE CHRISTIAN YEAR. Edited by Walter Lock, D.D. *Second Edition.*
THE IMITATION OF CHRIST. Edited by C. Bigg, D.D. *Fourth Edition.*
A BOOK OF DEVOTIONS. Edited by J. W. Stanbridge. B.D. *Second Edition.*
LYRA INNOCENTIUM. Edited by Walter Lock, D.D.
A SERIOUS CALL TO A DEVOUT AND HOLY LIFE. Edited by C. Bigg, D.D. *Second Edition.*
THE TEMPLE. Edited by E. C. S. Gibson, D.D.
A GUIDE TO ETERNITY. Edited by J. W. Stanbridge, B.D.
THE PSALMS OF DAVID. Edited by B. W. Randolph, D.D.
LYRA APOSTOLICA. Edited by Canon Scott Holland and Canon H. C. Beeching, M.A.
THE INNER WAY. By J. Tauler. Edited by A. W. Hutton, M.A.
THE THOUGHTS OF PASCAL. Edited by C. S. Jerram, M.A.
ON THE LOVE OF GOD. By St. Francis de Sales. Edited by W. J. Knox-Little, M.A.
A MANUAL OF CONSOLATION FROM THE SAINTS AND FATHERS. Edited by J. H. Burn, B.D.
THE SONG OF SONGS. Edited by B. Blaxland, M.A.
THE DEVOTIONS OF ST. ANSELM. Edited by C. C. J. Webb, M.A.
GRACE ABOUNDING. By John Bunyan. Edited by S. C. Freer, M.A.
BISHOP WILSON'S SACRA PRIVATA. Edited by A. E. Burn, B.D.
LYRA SACRA : A Book of Sacred Verse. Edited by H. C. Beeching, M.A, Canon of Westminster.
A DAY BOOK FROM THE SAINTS AND FATHERS. Edited by J. H. Burn, B.D.
HEAVENLY WISDOM. A Selection from the English Mystics. Edited by E. C. Gregory.
LIGHT, LIFE, and LOVE. A Selection from the German Mystics. Edited by W. R. Inge, M.A.

Illustrated Pocket Library of Plain and Coloured Books, The

Fcap 8vo. 3s. 6d. net each volume.

A series, in small form, of some of the famous illustrated books of fiction and general literature. These are faithfully reprinted from the first or best editions without introduction or notes.

COLOURED BOOKS

OLD COLOURED BOOKS. By George Paston. With 16 Coloured Plates. *Fcap. 8vo. 2s. net.*
THE LIFE AND DEATH OF JOHN MYTTON, ESQ. By Nimrod. With 18 Coloured Plates by Henry Alken and T. J. Rawlins. *Third Edition. 3s. 6d. net.*
Also a limited edition on large Japanese paper. *30s. net.*
THE LIFE OF A SPORTSMAN. By Nimrod. With 35 Coloured Plates by Henry Alken. *3s. 6d. net.*
Also a limited edition on large Japanese paper. *30s. net.*
HANDLEY CROSS. By R. S. SURTEES. With 17 Coloured Plates and 100 Woodcuts in the Text by John Leech. *3s. 6d. net.*
Also a limited edition on large Japanese paper. *30s. net.*
MR. SPONGE'S SPORTING TOUR. By R. S. Surtees. With 13 Coloured Plates and 90 Woodcuts in the Text by John Leech. *3s. 6d. net.*
Also a limited edition on large Japanese paper. *30s. net.*

JORROCKS' JAUNTS AND JOLLITIES. By R. S. Surtees. With 15 Coloured Plates by H. Alken. 3s. 6d. net.
  Also a limited edition on large Japanese paper. 30s. net.
  This volume is reprinted from the extremely rare and costly edition of 1843, which contains Alken's very fine illustrations instead of the usual ones by Phiz.
ASK MAMMA. By R. S. Surtees. With 13 Coloured Plates and 70 Woodcuts in the Text by John Leech. 3s. 6d. net.
  Also a limited edition on large Japanese paper. 30s. net.
THE ANALYSIS OF THE HUNTING FIELD. By R. S. Surtees. With 7 Coloured Plates by Henry Alken, and 43 Illustrations on Wood. 3s. 6d. net.
THE TOUR OF DR. SYNTAX IN SEARCH OF THE PICTURESQUE. By William Combe. With 30 Coloured Plates by T. Rowlandson. 3s. 6d. net.
  Also a limited edition on large Japanese paper. 30s. net.
THE TOUR OF DOCTOR SYNTAX IN SEARCH OF CONSOLATION. By William Combe. With 24 Coloured Plates by T. Rowlandson. 3s. 6d. net.
  Also a limited edition on large Japanese paper. 30s. net.
THE THIRD TOUR OF DOCTOR SYNTAX IN SEARCH OF A WIFE. By William Combe. With 24 Coloured Plates by T. Rowlandson. 3s. 6d. net.
  Also a limited edition on large Japanese paper. 30s. net.
THE HISTORY OF JOHNNY QUAE GENUS : the Little Foundling of the late Dr. Syntax. By the Author of 'The Three Tours.' With 24 Coloured Plates by Rowlandson. 3s. 6d. net.
  Also a limited edition on large Japanese paper. 30s. net.
THE ENGLISH DANCE OF DEATH, from the Designs of T. Rowlandson, with Metrical Illustrations by the Author of 'Doctor Syntax.' *Two Volumes.* 7s. net.
  This book contains 76 Coloured Plates.
  Also a limited edition on large Japanese paper. 30s. net.
THE DANCE OF LIFE: A Poem. By the Author of 'Doctor Syntax.' Illustrated with 26 Coloured Engravings by T. Rowlandson. 3s. 6d. net.
  Also a limited edition on large Japanese paper. 30s. net.
LIFE IN LONDON : or, the Day and Night Scenes of Jerry Hawthorn, Esq., and his Elegant Friend, Corinthian Tom. By Pierce Egan. With 36 Coloured Plates by I. R. and G. Cruikshank. With numerous Designs on Wood. 3s. 6d. net.
  Also a limited edition on large Japanese paper. 30s. net.
*REAL LIFE IN LONDON : or, the Rambles and Adventures of Bob Tallyho, Esq., and his Cousin, The Hon. Tom Dashall. By an Amateur (Pierce Egan). With 31 Coloured Plates by Alken and Rowlandson, etc. *Two Volumes.* 7s. net.
THE LIFE OF AN ACTOR. By Pierce Egan. With 27 Coloured Plates by Theodore Lane, and several Designs on Wood. 3s. 6d. net.
THE VICAR OF WAKEFIELD. By Oliver Goldsmith. With 24 Coloured Plates by T. Rowlandson. 3s. 6d. net.
  Also a limited edition on large Japenese paper. 30s. net.
  A reproduction of a very rare book.
THE MILITARY ADVENTURES OF JOHNNY NEWCOME. By an Officer. With 15 Coloured Plates by T. Rowlandson. 3s. 6d. net.
THE NATIONAL SPORTS OF GREAT BRITAIN. With Descriptions and 51 Coloured Plates by Henry Alken. 3s. 6d. net.
  Also a limited edition on large Japanese paper. 30s. net.
  This book is completely different from the large folio edition of 'National Sports' by the same artist, and none of the plates are similar.
THE ADVENTURES OF A POST CAPTAIN. By A Naval Officer. With 24 Coloured Plates by Mr. Williams. 3s. 6d. net.
GAMONIA : or, the Art of Preserving Game ; and an Improved Method of making Plantations and Covers, explained and illustrated by Lawrence Rawstorne, Esq. With 15 Coloured Plates by T. Rawlins. 3s. 6d. net.
AN ACADEMY FOR GROWN HORSEMEN : Containing the completest Instructions for Walking, Trotting, Cantering, Galloping, Stumbling, and Tumbling. Illustrated with 27 Coloured Plates, and adorned with a Portrait of the Author. By Geoffrey Gambado, Esq. 3s. 6d. net.
REAL LIFE IN IRELAND, or, the Day and Night Scenes of Brian Boru, Esq., and his Elegant Friend, Sir Shawn O'Dogherty. By a Real Paddy. With 19 Coloured Plates by Heath, Marks, etc. 3s. 6d. net.
THE ADVENTURES OF JOHNNY NEWCOME IN THE NAVY. By Alfred Burton. With 16 Coloured Plates by T. Rowlandson 3s. 6d. net.
*THE OLD ENGLISH SQUIRE: A Poem. By John Careless, Esq. With 20 Coloured Plates after the style of T. Rowlandson.

PLAIN BOOKS

THE GRAVE: A Poem. By Robert Blair. Illustrated by 12 Etchings executed by Louis Schiavonetti from the original Inventions of William Blake. With an Engraved Title Page and a Portrait of Blake by T. Phillips, R.A. 3*s.* 6*d. net.*

The illustrations are reproduced in photogravure. Also a limited edition on large Japanese paper, with India proofs and a duplicate set of the plates. 15*s. net.*

ILLUSTRATIONS OF THE BOOK OF JOB. Invented and engraved by William Blake. 3*s.* 6*d. net.*

These famous Illustrations—21 in number—are reproduced in photogravure. Also a limited edition on large Japanese paper, with India proofs and a duplicate set of the plates. 15*s. net.*

ÆSOP'S FABLES. With 380 Woodcuts by Thomas Bewick. 3*s.* 6*d. net.*

WINDSOR CASTLE. By W. Harrison Ainsworth. With 22 Plates and 87 Woodcuts in the Text by George Cruikshank. 3*s.* 6*d. net.*

THE TOWER OF LONDON. By W. Harrison Ainsworth. With 40 Plates and 58 Woodcuts in the Text by George Cruikshank. 3*s.* 6*d. net.*

FRANK FAIRLEGH. By F. E. Smedley. With 30 Plates by George Cruikshank. 3*s.* 6*d. net.*

HANDY ANDY. By Samuel Lover. With 24 Illustrations by the Author. 3*s.* 6*d. net.*

THE COMPLEAT ANGLER. By Izaak Walton and Charles Cotton. With 14 Plates and 77 Woodcuts in the Text. 3*s.* 6*d. net.*

This volume is reproduced from the beautiful edition of John Major of 1824.

THE PICKWICK PAPERS. By Charles Dickens. With the 43 Illustrations by Seymour and Phiz, the two Buss Plates, and the 32 Contemporary Onwhyn Plates. 3*s.* 6*d. net.*

Junior Examination Series

Edited by A. M. M. STEDMAN, M.A. *Fcap.* 8*vo.* 1*s.*

This series is intended to lead up to the School Examination Series, and is intended for the use of teachers and students, to supply material for the former and practice for the latter. The papers are carefully graduated, cover the whole of the subject usually taught, and are intended to form part of the ordinary class work. They may be used *vivâ voce* or as a written examination.

JUNIOR FRENCH EXAMINATION PAPERS. By F. Jacob, M.A.

JUNIOR LATIN EXAMINATION PAPERS. By C. G. Botting, M.A. *Third Edition.*

JUNIOR ENGLISH EXAMINATION PAPERS. By W. Williamson, M.A.

JUNIOR ARITHMETIC EXAMINATION PAPERS. By W. S. Beard. *Second Edition.*

JUNIOR ALGEBRA EXAMINATION PAPERS. By S. W. Finn, M.A.

JUNIOR GREEK EXAMINATION PAPERS. By T. C. Weatherhead, M.A.

JUNIOR GENERAL INFORMATION EXAMINATION PAPERS. By W. S. Beard.

JUNIOR GEOGRAPHY EXAMINATION PAPERS. By W. G. Baker, M.A.

JUNIOR GERMAN EXAMINATION PAPERS. By A. Voegelin, M.A.

Junior School-Books, Methuen's

Edited by O. D. INSKIP, LL.D., and W. WILLIAMSON, B.A.

A series of elementary books for pupils in lower forms, simply written by teachers of experience.

A CLASS-BOOK OF DICTATION PASSAGES. By W. Williamson, B.A. *Tenth Edition.* Cr. 8*vo.* 1*s.* 6*d.*

THE GOSPEL ACCORDING TO ST. MATTHEW. Edited by E. Wilton South, M.A. With Three aps. *Crown* 8*vo.* 1*s.* 6*d.*

THE GOSPEL ACCORDING TO ST. MARK. Edited by A. E. Rubie, D.D. With Three Maps. *Crown* 8*vo.* 1*s.* 6*d.*

A JUNIOR ENGLISH GRAMMAR. By W. Williamson, B.A. With numerous passages for parsing and analysis, and a chapter on Essay Writing. *Second Edition. Crown* 8*vo.* 2*s.*

A JUNIOR CHEMISTRY. By E. A. Tyler, B.A., F.C.S. With 73 Illustrations. *Second Edition. Crown* 8*vo.* 2*s.* 6*d.*

THE ACTS OF THE APOSTLES. Edited by A. E. Rubie, D.D. *Crown* 8*vo.* 2*s.*

A JUNIOR FRENCH GRAMMAR. By L. A. Sornet and M. J. Acatos. *Crown* 8*vo.* 2*s.*

ELEMENTARY EXPERIMENTAL SCIENCE. PHYSICS by W. T. Clough, A.R.C.S. CHEMISTRY by A. E. Dunstan, B.Sc. With 2 Plates and 154 Diagrams. *Crown* 8*vo.* 2*s.* 6*d.*

A JUNIOR GEOMETRY. By Noel S. Lydon. With 230 Diagrams. *Crown* 8*vo.* 2*s.*

*A JUNIOR MAGNETISM AND ELECTRICITY. By W. T. CLOUGH. With many Illustrations. *Crown* 8*vo.* 2*s.* 6*d.*

*ELEMENTARY EXPERIMENTAL CHEMISTRY. By A. E. Dunstan, B.Sc. With many Illustrations. *Crown* 8*vo.* 2*s.*

*A JUNIOR FRENCH PROSE. By R. R. N. Baron, M.A. *Crown* 8*vo.* 2*s.*

*THE GOSPEL ACCORDING TO ST. LUKE. With an Introduction and Notes by William Williamson, B.A. With Three Maps. *Crown* 8*vo.* 1*s.* 6*d.*

Leaders of Religion

Edited by H. C. BEECHING, M.A., Canon of Westminster. *With Portraits.*
Crown 8vo. 2s. net.

A series of short biographies of the most prominent leaders of religious life and thought of all ages and countries.

CARDINAL NEWMAN. By R. H. Hutton.
JOHN WESLEY. By J. H. Overton, M.A.
BISHOP WILBERFORCE. By G. W. Daniell, M.A.
CARDINAL MANNING. By A. W. Hutton, M.A.
CHARLES SIMEON. By H. C. G. Moule, D.D.
JOHN KEBLE. By Walter Lock, D.D.
THOMAS CHALMERS. By Mrs. Oliphant.
LANCELOT ANDREWES. By R. L. Ottley, D.D. *Second Edition.*
AUGUSTINE OF CANTERBURY. By E. L. Cutts, D.D.

WILLIAM LAUD. By W. H. Hutton, M.A. *Second Edition.*
JOHN KNOX. By F. MacCunn. *Second Edition.*
JOHN HOWE. By R. F. Horton, D.D.
BISHOP KEN. By F. A. Clarke, M.A.
GEORGE FOX, THE QUAKER. By T. Hodgkin, D.C.L.
JOHN DONNE. By Augustus Jessopp, D.D.
THOMAS CRANMER. By A. J. Mason, D.D.
BISHOP LATIMER. By R. M. Carlyle and A. J. Carlyle, M.A.
BISHOP BUTLER. By W. A. Spooner, M.A.

Little Blue Books, The

General Editor, E. V. LUCAS.
Illustrated. Demy 16mo. 2s. 6d.

A series of books for children. The aim of the editor is to get entertaining or exciting stories about normal children, the moral of which is implied rather than expressed.

1. THE CASTAWAYS OF MEADOWBANK. By Thomas Cobb.
2. THE BEECHNUT BOOK. By Jacob Abbott. Edited by E. V. Lucas.
3. THE AIR GUN. By T. Hilbert.
4. A SCHOOL YEAR. By Netta Syrett.
5. THE PEELES AT THE CAPITAL. By Roger Ashton.
6. THE TREASURE OF PRINCEGATE PRIORY. By T. Cobb.
7. Mrs. BARBERRY'S GENERAL SHOP. By Roger Ashton.
8. A BOOK OF BAD CHILDREN. By W. T. Webb.
9. THE LOST BALL. By Thomas Cobb.

Little Books on Art

With many Illustrations. Demy 16mo. 2s. 6d. net.

A series of monographs in miniature, containing the complete outline of the subject under treatment and rejecting minute details. These books are produced with the greatest care. Each volume consists of about 200 pages, and contains from 30 to 40 illustrations, including a frontispiece in photogravure.

GREEK ART. H. B. Walters.
BOOKPLATES. E. Almack.
REYNOLDS. J. Sime.
ROMNEY. George Paston.
WATTS. Miss R. E. D. Sketchley.
LEIGHTON. Alice Corkran.
VELASQUEZ. Wilfrid Wilberforce and A. R. Gilbert.
GREUZE AND BOUCHER. Eliza F. Pollard.
VANDYCK. M. G. Smallwood.

TURNER. F. Tyrell-Gill.
DÜRER. Jessie Allen.
HOPPNER. H. P. K. Skipton.
HOLBEIN. Mrs. G. Fortescue.
BURNE-JONES. Fortunée de Lisle.
REMBRANDT. Mrs. E. A. Sharp.
COROT. Alice Pollard and Ethel Birnstingl.
MILLET. Netta Peacock.
*RAPHAEL. A. R. Dryhurst.
*ILLUMINATED MSS. J. W. Bradley.

Little Galleries, The

Demy 16mo. 2s. 6d. net.

A series of little books containing examples of the best work of the great painters. Each volume contains 20 plates in photogravure, together with a short outline of the life and work of the master to whom the book is devoted.

A LITTLE GALLERY OF REYNOLDS.
A LITTLE GALLERY OF ROMNEY.
A LITTLE GALLERY OF HOPPNER.
A LITTLE GALLERY OF MILLAIS.
A LITTLE GALLERY OF ENGLISH POETS.

Little Guides, The
Small Pott 8vo, cloth, 2s. 6d. net.; leather, 3s. 6d. net.

OXFORD AND ITS COLLEGES. By J. Wells, M.A. Illustrated by E. H. New. *Fourth Edition.*

CAMBRIDGE AND ITS COLLEGES. By A. Hamilton Thompson. *Second Edition.* Illustrated by E. H. New.

THE MALVERN COUNTRY. By B. C. A. Windle, D.Sc., F.R.S. Illustrated by E. H. New.

SHAKESPEARE'S COUNTRY. By B. C. A. Windle, D.Sc., F.R.S. Illustrated by E. H. New. *Second Edition.*

SUSSEX. By F. G. Brabant, M.A. Illustrated by E. H. New.

WESTMINSTER ABBEY. By G. E. Troutbeck. Illustrated by F. D. Bedford.

NORFOLK. By W A. Dutt. Illustrated by B. C. Boulter.

CORNWALL. By A. L. Salmon. Illustrated by B. C. Boulter.

BRITTANY. By S. Baring-Gould. Illustrated by J. Wylie.

HERTFORDSHIRE. By H. W. Tompkins, F.R.H.S. Illustrated by E. H. New.

THE ENGLISH LAKES. By F. G. Brabant, M.A. Illustrated by E. H. New.

KENT. By G. Clinch. Illustrated by F. D. Bedford.

ROME By C. G. Ellaby. Illustrated by B. C. Boulter.

THE ISLE OF WIGHT. By G. Clinch. Illustrated by F. D. Bedford.

SURREY. By F. A. H. Lambert. Illustrated by E. H. New.

BUCKINGHAMSHIRE. By E. S. Roscoe. Illustrated by F. D. Bedford.

SUFFOLK. By W. A. Dutt. Illustrated by J. Wylie.

DERBYSHIRE. By J. C. Cox, LL.D., F.S.A. Illustrated by J. C. Wall.

THE NORTH RIDING OF YORKSHIRE. By J. E. Morris. Illustrated by R. J. S. Bertram.

HAMPSHIRE. By J. C. Cox. Illustrated by M. E. Purser.

SICILY. By F. H. Jackson. With many Illustrations by the Author.

*DORSET. By Frank R. Heath. Illustrated.

*CHESHIRE. By W. M. Gallichan. Illustrated by Elizabeth Hartley.

Little Library, The
With Introductions, Notes, and Photogravure Frontispieces.

Small Pott 8vo. Each Volume, cloth, 1s. 6d. net; leather, 2s. 6d. net.

A series of small books under the above title, containing some of the famous works in English and other literatures, in the domains of fiction, poetry, and belles lettres. The series also contains volumes of selections in prose and verse.

The books are edited with the most sympathetic and scholarly care. Each one contains an introduction which gives (1) a short biography of the author; (2) a critical estimate of the book. Where they are necessary, short notes are added at the foot of the page.

Each volume has a photogravure frontispiece, and the books are produced with great care.

ENGLISH LYRICS, A LITTLE BOOK OF. Anon.

PRIDE AND PREJUDICE. By Jane Austen. Edited by E. V. Lucas. *Two Volumes.*

NORTHANGER ABBEY. By Jane Austen. Edited by E. V. Lucas.

THE ESSAYS OF LORD BACON. Edited by Edward Wright.

THE INGOLSBY LEGENDS. By R. H. Barham. Edited by J. B. Atlay. *Two Volumes.*

A LITTLE BOOK OF ENGLISH PROSE. Edited by Mrs. P. A. Barnett.

THE HISTORY OF THE CALIPH VATHEK. By William Beckford. Edited by E. Denison Ross.

SELECTIONS FROM WILLIAM BLAKE. Edited by M. Perugini.

LAVENGRO. By George Borrow. Edited by F. Hindes Groome. *Two Volumes.*

THE ROMANY RYE. By George Borrow. Edited by John Sampson.

SELECTIONS FROM THE EARLY POEMS OF ROBERT BROWNING. Edited by W. Hall Griffin, M.A.

SELECTIONS FROM THE ANTI-JACOBIN; with George Canning's additional Poems. Edited by Lloyd Sanders.

THE ESSAYS OF ABRAHAM COWLEY. Edited by H. C. Minchin.

SELECTIONS FROM GEORGE CRABBE. Edited by A. C. Deane.

JOHN HALIFAX GENTLEMAN. By Mrs. Craik. Edited by Annie Matheson. *Two Volumes.*

THE ENGLISH POEMS OF RICHARD CRAWSHAW. Edited by Edward Hutton.

THE INFERNO OF DANTE. Translated by H. F. Cary. Edited by Paget Toynbee, M.A., D.Litt.

THE PURGATORIO OF DANTE. Translated by H. F. Cary. Edited by Paget Toynbee, M.A. D.Litt.

THE PARADISO OF DANTE. Translated by H. F. Cary. Edited by Paget Toynbee, M.A., D.Litt.
SELECTIONS FROM THE POEMS OF GEORGE DARLEY. Edited by R. A. Streatfeild.
A LITTLE BOOK OF LIGHT VERSE. Edited by A C. Deane.
MARRIAGE. By Susan Ferrier. Edited by Miss Goodrich Freer and Lord Iddesleigh. *Two Volumes.*
THE INHERITANCE. By Susan Ferrier. Edited by Miss Goodrich Freer and Lord Iddesleigh. *Two Volumes.*
CRANFORD. By Mrs. Gaskell. Edited by E. V. Lucas. *Second Edition.*
THE SCARLET LETTER. By Nathaniel Hawthorne. Edited by Percy Dearmer.
A LITTLE BOOK OF SCOTTISH VERSE. Edited by T. F. Henderson.
POEMS. By John Keats. With an Introduction by L. Binyon and Notes by J. MASEFIELD.
EOTHEN. By A. W. Kinglake. With an Introduction and Notes. *Second Edition.*
ELIA, AND THE LAST ESSAYS OF ELIA. By Charles Lamb. Edited by E. V. Lucas.
LONDON LYRICS. By F. Locker. Edited by A. D. Godley, M.A.
    A reprint of the First Edition.
SELECTIONS FROM LONGFELLOW. Edited by L. M. Faithfull.
THE POEMS OF ANDREW MARVELL. Edited by E. Wright.
THE MINOR POEMS OF JOHN MILTON. Edited by H. C. BEECHING, M.A.
MANSIE WAUCH. By D. M. Moir. Edited by T. F. Henderson.
A LITTLE BOOK OF ENGLISH SONNETS. Edited by J. B. B. Nichols.
THE MAXIMS OF LA ROCHEFOUCAULD. Translated by Dean Stanhope. Edited by G. H. Powell.
REJECTED ADDRESSES. By Horace and James Smith. Edited by A. D. Godley, M.A.
A SENTIMENTAL JOURNEY. By Laurence Sterne. Edited by H. W. Paul.
THE EARLY POEMS OF ALFRED, LORD TENNYSON. Edited by J. Churton Collins, M.A.
IN MEMORIAM. By Alfred, Lord Tennyson. Edited by H. C. Beeching, M.A.
THE PRINCESS. By Alfred, Lord Tennyson. Edited by Elizabeth Wordsworth.
MAUD. By Alfred, Lord Tennyson. Edited by Elizabeth Wordsworth.
VANITY FAIR. By W. M. Thackeray. Edited by S. Gywnn. *Three Volumes.*
PENDENNIS. By W. M. Thackeray. Edited by S. Gwynn. *Three Volumes.*
ESMOND. By W. M. Thackeray. Edited by S. Gwynn.
CHRISTMAS BOOKS. By W. M. Thackeray. Edited by S. Gwynn.
THE POEMS OF HENRY VAUGHAN. Edited by Edward Hutton.
THE COMPLEAT ANGLER. By Izaak Walton. Edited by J. Buchan.
A LITTLE BOOK OF LIFE AND DEATH. Edited by Mrs. Alfred Waterhouse. *Sixth Edition.*
SELECTIONS FROM WORDSWORTH. Edited by Nowell C. Smith.
LYRICAL BALLADS. By W. Wordsworth and S. T. Coleridge. Edited by George Sampson.

Miniature Library, Methuen's

Reprints in miniature of a few interesting books which have qualities of humanity, devotion, or literary genius.

EUPHRANOR: A Dialogue on Youth. By Edward FitzGerald. From the edition published by W. Pickering in 1851. *Demy 32mo. Leather, 2s. net.*
POLONIUS: or Wise Saws and Modern Instances. By Edward FitzGerald. From the edition published by W. Pickering in 1852. *Demy 32mo. Leather, 2s. net.*
THE RUBAIYAT OF OMAR KHAYYAM. By Edward FitzGerald. From the 1st edition of 1859, *Second Edition. Leather, 2s. net.*
THE LIFE OF EDWARD, LORD HERBERT OF CHERBURY. Written by himself. From the edition printed at Strawberry Hill in the year 1764. *Medium 32mo. Leather, 2s. net.*
THE VISIONS OF DOM FRANCISCO QUEVEDO VILLEGAS, Knight of the Order of St. James Made English by R. L. From the edition printed for H. Herringman 1668. *Leather. 2s. net.*
POEMS. By Dora Greenwell. From the edition of 1848. *Leather, 2s. net.*

The Oxford Biographies

Fcap. 8vo.   Each volume, cloth, 2s. 6d. net ; leather, 3s. 6d. net.

These books are written by scholars of repute, who combine knowledge and literary skill with the power of popular presentation. They are illustrated from authentic material.

DANTE ALIGHIERI. By Paget Toynbee, M.A., D.Litt. With 12 Illustrations. *Second Edition.*
SAVONAROLA. By E. L. S. Horsburgh, M.A. With 12 Illustrations. *Second Edition.*
JOHN HOWARD. By E. C. S. Gibson, D.D., Vicar of Leeds. With 12 Illustrations.

TENNYSON. By A. C. BENSON, M.A. With 9 Illustrations.
WALTER RALEIGH. By I. A. Taylor. With 12 Illustrations.
ERASMUS. By E. F. H. Capey. With 12 Illustrations.
THE YOUNG PRETENDER. By C. S. Terry. With 12 Illustrations.
ROBERT BURNS. By T. F. Henderson. With 12 Illustrations.
CHATHAM. By A. S. M'Dowall. With 12 Illustrations.
ST. FRANCIS OF ASSISI. By Anna M. Stoddart. With 16 Illustrations.
CANNING. By W. A. Phillips. With 12 Illustrations.
BEACONSFIELD. By Walter Sichel. With 12 Illustrations.
GOETHE. By H. G. Atkins. With 12 Illustrations.

School Examination Series

Edited by A. M. M. STEDMAN, M.A. *Crown 8vo.* 2s. 6d.

FRENCH EXAMINATION PAPERS. By A. M. M. Stedman, M.A. *Thirteenth Edition.*
   A KEY, issued to Tutors and Private Students only to be had on application to the
   Publishers. *Fifth Edition. Crown 8vo.* 6s. net.
LATIN EXAMINATION PAPERS. By A. M. M. Stedman, M.A. *Twelfth Edition.*
   KEY (*Fourth Edition*) issued as above. 6s. net.
GREEK EXAMINATION PAPERS. By A. M. M. Stedman, M.A. *Seventh Edition.*
   KEY (*Second Edition*) issued as above. 6s. net.
GERMAN EXAMINATION PAPERS. By R. J. Morich. *Fifth Edition.*
   KEY (*Second Edition*) issued as above. 6s. net.
HISTORY AND GEOGRAPHY EXAMINATION PAPERS. By C. H. Spence, M.A. *Second Edition.*
PHYSICS EXAMINATION PAPERS. By R. E. Steel, M.A., F.C.S.
GENERAL KNOWLEDGE EXAMINATION PAPERS. By A. M. M. Stedman, M.A. *Fourth Edition.*
   KEY (*Third Edition*) issued as above. 7s. net.
EXAMINATION PAPERS IN ENGLISH HISTORY. By J. Tait Plowden-Wardlaw, B.A.

Social Questions of To-day

Edited by H. DE B. GIBBINS, Litt.D., M.A. *Crown 8vo.* 2s. 6d.

A series of volumes upon those topics of social, economic, and industrial interest
that are foremost in the public mind.

Each volume is written by an author who is an acknowledged authority upon the
subject with which he deals.

TRADE UNIONISM—NEW AND OLD. By G. Howell. *Third Edition.*
THE CO-OPERATIVE MOVEMENT TO-DAY. By G. J. Holyoake. *Fourth Edition.*
MUTUAL THRIFT. By J. Frome Wilkinson, M.A.
PROBLEMS OF POVERTY. By J. A. Hobson, M.A. *Fourth Edition.*
THE COMMERCE OF NATIONS. By C. F. Bastable, M.A. *Third Edition.*
THE ALIEN INVASION. By W. H. Wilkins, B.A.
THE RURAL EXODUS. By P. Anderson Graham.
LAND NATIONALIZATION. By Harold Cox, B.A.
A SHORTER WORKING DAY, By H. de Gibbins and R. A. Hadfield.
BACK TO THE LAND. An Inquiry into Rural Depopulation. By H. E. Moore.
TRUSTS, POOLS, AND CORNERS. By J. Stephen Jeans.
THE FACTORY SYSTEM. By R. W. Cooke-Taylor.
THE STATE AND ITS CHILDREN. By Gertrude Tuckwell.
WOMEN'S WORK. By Lady Dilke, Miss Bulley, and Miss Whitley.
SOCIALISM AND MODERN THOUGHT. By M. Kauffmann.
THE PROBLEM OF THE UNEMPLOYED. By J. A. Hobson, M.A.
LIFE IN WEST LONDON. By Arthur Sherwell, M.A. *Third Edition.*
RAILWAY NATIONALIZATION. By Clement Edwards.
WORKHOUSES AND PAUPERISM. By Louisa Twining.
UNIVERSITY AND SOCIAL SETTLEMENTS. By W. Reason, M.A.

Technology, Textbooks of

Edited by PROFESSOR J. WERTHEIMER, F.I.C.
Fully Illustrated.

HOW TO MAKE A DRESS. By J. A. E. Wood. *Third Edition. Crown 8vo.* 1s. 6d.
CARPENTRY AND JOINERY. By F. C. Webber. *Third Edition. Crown 8vo.* 3s. 6d.
PRACTICAL MECHANICS. By Sidney H. Wells. *Second Edition. Crown 8vo.* 3s. 6d.

PRACTICAL PHYSICS. By H. Stroud, D.Sc., M.A. *Crown 8vo. 3s. 6d.*
MILLINERY, THEORETICAL AND PRACTICAL. By Clare Hill. *Second Edition. Crown 8vo. 2s.*
PRACTICAL CHEMISTRY. Part I. By W. French, M.A. *Crown 8vo. Second Edition. 1s. 6d.*
PRACTICAL CHEMISTRY. Part II. By W. French, M.A., and T. H. Boardman, M.A.
  Crown 8vo. 1s. 6d.
TECHNICAL ARITHMETIC AND GEOMETRY. By C. T. Millis, M.I.M.E. *Crown 8vo. 3s. 6d.*
AN INTRODUCTION TO THE STUDY OF TEXTILE DESIGN. By Aldred F. Barker. *Demy 8vo.
  7s. 6d.*
BUILDERS' QUANTITIES. By H. C. Grubb. *Crown 8vo. 4s. 6d.*
*METAL WORK (REPOUSSÉ). By A. C. Horth. *Crown 8vo. 3s. 6d.*

Theology, Handbooks of

Edited by R. L. OTTLEY, D.D., Professor of Pastoral Theology at Oxford,
and Canon of Christ Church, Oxford.

The series is intended, in part, to furnish the clergy and teachers or students of
Theology with trustworthy Text-books, adequately representing the present position
of the questions dealt with; in part, to make accessible to the reading public an
accurate and concise statement of facts and principles in all questions bearing on
Theology and Religion.

THE XXXIX. ARTICLES OF THE CHURCH OF ENGLAND. Edited by E. C. S. Gibson, D.D.
  Third and Cheaper Edition in one Volume. Demy 8vo. 12s. 6d.
AN INTRODUCTION TO THE HISTORY OF RELIGION. By F. B. Jevons, M.A., Litt.D. *Third
  Edition. Demy 8vo. 10s. 6d.*
THE DOCTRINE OF THE INCARNATION. By R. L. Ottley, D.D. *Second and Cheaper Edition.
  Demy 8vo. 12s. 6d.*
AN INTRODUCTION TO THE HISTORY OF THE CREEDS. By A. E. Burn, B.D. *Demy 8vo.
  10s. 6d.*
THE PHILOSOPHY OF RELIGION IN ENGLAND AND AMERICA. By Alfred Caldecott, D.D.
  Demy 8vo. 10s. 6d.
A HISTORY OF EARLY CHRISTIAN DOCTRINE. By J. F. Bethune Baker, M.A. *Demy 8vo.
  10s. 6d.*

Methuen's Universal Library

EDITED BY SIDNEY LEE. *In Sixpenny Volumes.*

MESSRS. METHUEN are preparing a new series of reprints containing both books of classical
repute, which are accessible in various forms, and also some rarer books, of which no satisfactory
edition at a moderate price is in existence. It is their ambition to place the best books of all
nations, and particularly of the Anglo-Saxon race, within the reach of every reader. All the
great masters of Poetry, Drama, Fiction, History, Biography, and Philosophy will be represented. Mr. Sidney Lee will be the General Editor of the Library, and he will contribute a
Note to each book.

The characteristics of METHUEN'S UNIVERSAL LIBRARY are five :—
  1. SOUNDNESS OF TEXT. A pure and unabridged text is the primary object of the series,
and the books will be carefully reprinted under the direction of competent scholars from the
best editions. In a series intended for popular use not less than for students, adherence to the
old spelling would in many cases leave the matter unintelligible to ordinary readers, and, as the
appeal of a classic is universal, the spelling has in general been modernised.
  2. COMPLETENESS. Where it seems advisable, the complete works of such masters as Milton
Bacon, Ben Jonson and Sir Thomas Browne will be given. These will be issued in separate
volumes, so that the reader who does not desire all the works of an author will have the oppor-
tunity of acquiring a single masterpiece.
  3. CHEAPNESS. The books will be well printed on good paper at a price which on the whole
is without parallel in the history of publishing. Each volume will contain from 100 to 350 pages,
and will be issued in paper covers, Crown 8vo, at Sixpence net. In a few cases a long book will
be issued as a Double Volume at One Shilling net.
  4. CLEARNESS OF TYPE. The type will be a very legible one.
  5. SIMPLICITY. There will be no editorial matter except a short biographical and biblio-
graphical note by Mr. Sidney Lee at the beginning of each volume.

The volumes may also be obtained in cloth at One Shilling net, or in the case of a Double
Volume at One and Sixpence net. Thus TOM JONES may be bought in a Double paper volume
at One Shilling net, or in one cloth volume at 1s. 6d. net.

The Library will be issued at regular intervals after the publication of the first six books, all
of which will be published together. Due notice will be given of succeeding issues. The orders

of publication will be arranged to give as much variety of subject as possible, and the volume composing the complete works of an author will be issued at convenient intervals.

These are the early Books, all of which are in the Press.

THE WORKS OF WILLIAM SHAKESPEARE. In 10 volumes.

VOL. I.—The Tempest; The Two Gentlemen of Verona; The Merry Wives of Windsor; Measure for Measure; The Comedy of Errors.

VOL. II.—Much Ado About Nothing; Love's Labour's Lost; A Midsummer Nights' Dream; The Merchant of Venice; As You Like It.

VOL. III.—The Taming of the Shrew; All's Well that Ends Well; Twelfth Night; The Winter's Tale.

THE PILGRIM'S PROGRESS. By John Bunyan.

THE NOVELS OF JANE AUSTEN. In 5 volumes.

VOL. I.—Sense and Sensibility.

THE ENGLISH WORKS OF FRANCIS BACON, LORD VERULAM.

Vol. I.—Essays and Counsels and the New Atlantis.

THE POEMS AND PLAYS OF OLIVER GOLDSMITH.

ON THE IMITATION OF CHRIST. By Thomas à Kempis.

THE WORKS OF BEN JOHNSON. In about 12 volumes.

VOL. I.—The Case is Altered; Every Man in His Humour; Every Man out of His Humour.

THE PROSE WORKS OF JOHN MILTON.

VOL. I.—Eikonoklastes and The Tenure of Kings and Magistrates.

SELECT WORKS OF EDMUND BURKE.

Vol. I.—Reflections on the French Revolution

Vol. II.—Speeches on America.

THE WORKS OF HENRY FIELDING.

Vol. I.—Tom Jones. (Double Volume.)

Vol. II.—Amelia. (Double Volume.)

THE POEMS OF THOMAS CHATTERTON. In 2 volumes.

Vol. I.—Miscellaneous Poems.

Vol. II.—The Rowley Poems.

THE MEDITATIONS OF MARCUS AURELIUS. Translated by R. Graves.

THE HISTORY OF THE DECLINE AND FALL OF THE ROMAN EMPIRE. By Edward Gibbon. In 7 volumes.

The Notes have been revised by J. B. Bury, Litt.D.

THE PLAYS OF CHRISTOPHER MARLOWE.

Vol. I.—Tamburlane the Great; The Tragical History of Doctor Faustus.

Vol. II.—The Jew of Malta: Edward the Second; The Massacre at Paris; The Tragedy of Dido.

THE NATURAL HISTORY AND ANTIQUITIES OF SELBORNE. By Gilbert White.

THE COMPLETE ANGLER. In 2 volumes.

Vol. I.—By Izaak Walton.

Vol. II.—Part 2, by Cotton, and Part 3 by Venables.

THE POEMS OF PERCY BYSSHE SHELLEY. In 4 volumes.

Vol. I.—Alastor; The Daemon of the World; The Revolt of Islam, etc.

THE WORKS OF SIR THOMAS BROWNE. In 6 volumes.

Vol. I.—Religio Medici and Urn Burial.

THE POEMS OF JOHN MILTON. In 2 volumes.

Vol. I.—Paradise Lost.

Vol. II.—Miscellaneous Poems and Paradise Regained.

HUMPHREY CLINKER. By T. G. Smollett.

SELECT WORKS OF SIR THOMAS MORE.

Vol. I.—Utopia and Poems.

THE ANALOGY OF RELIGION, NATURAL AND REVEALED. By Joseph Butler, D.D.

ON HUMAN UNDERSTANDING. By John Locke. In 3 volumes.

THE POEMS OF JOHN KEATS. In 2 volumes.

THE DIVINE COMEDY OF DANTE. The Italian Text edited by Paget Toynbee, M.A., D.Litt. (A Double Volume.)

Westminster Commentaries, The

General Editor, WALTER LOCK, D.D., Warden of Keble College, Dean Ireland's Professor of Exegesis in the University of Oxford.

The object of each commentary is primarily exegetical, to interpret the author's meaning to the present generation. The editors will not deal, except very subordinately, with questions of textual criticism or philology; but, taking the English text in the Revised Version as their basis, they will try to combine a hearty acceptance of critical principles with loyalty to the Catholic Faith.

THE BOOK OF GENESIS. Edited with Introduction and Notes by S. R. Driver, D.D. *Third Edition Demy 8vo. 10s. 6d.*

THE BOOK OF JOB. Edited by E. C. S. Gibson. D.D. *Second Edition. Demy 8vo. 6s.*

THE ACTS OF THE APOSTLES. Edited by R. B. Rackham, M.A. *Demy 8vo. Second and Cheaper Edition. 10s. 6d.*

THE FIRST EPISTLE OF PAUL THE APOSTLE TO THE CORINTHIANS. Edited by H. L. Goudge, M.A. *Demy 8vo. 6s.*

THE EPISTLE OF ST. JAMES. Edited with Introduction and Notes by R. J. Knowling, M.A. *Demy 8vo. 6s.*

PART II.—FICTION
Marie Corelli's Novels
Crown 8vo. 6s. each.

A ROMANCE OF TWO WORLDS. *Twenty-Fifth Edition.*
VENDETTA. *Twenty-First Edition.*
THELMA. *Thirty-First Edition.*
ARDATH: THE STORY OF A DEAD SELF. *Fifteenth Edition.*
THE SOUL OF LILITH. *Twelfth Edition.*
WORMWOOD. *Fourteenth Edition.*
BARABBAS: A DREAM OF THE WORLD'S TRAGEDY. *Thirty-Ninth Edition.*
'The tender reverence of the treatment and the imaginative beauty of the writing have reconciled us to the daring of the conception. This "Dream of the World's Tragedy" is a lofty and not inadequate paraphrase of the supreme climax of the inspired narrative.'—*Dublin Review.*
THE SORROWS OF SATAN. *Forty-Eighth Edition.*
'A very powerful piece of work. . . . The conception is magnificent, and is likely to win an abiding place within the memory of man. . . . The author has immense command of language, and a limitless audacity. . . . This interesting and remarkable romance will live long after much of the ephemeral literature of the day is forgotten. . . . A literary phenomenon . . . novel, and even sublime.'—W. T. STEAD in the *Review of Reviews.*
THE MASTER CHRISTIAN. [*165th Thousand.*
'It cannot be denied that "The Master Christian" is a powerful book; that it is one likely to raise uncomfortable questions in all but the most self-satisfied readers, and that it strikes at the root of the failure of the Churches—the decay of faith—in a manner which shows the inevitable disaster heaping up . . . The good Cardinal Bonpré is a beautiful figure, fit to stand beside the good Bishop in "Les Misérables." It is a book with a serious purpose expressed with absolute unconventionality and passion . . . And this is to say it is a book worth reading.'—*Examiner.*
TEMPORAL POWER: A STUDY IN SUPREMACY. [*150th Thousand.*
'It is impossible to read such a work as "Temporal Power" without becoming convinced that the story is intended to convey certain criticisms on the ways of the world and certain suggestions for the betterment of humanity. . . . If the chief intention of the book was to hold the mirror up to shams, injustice, dishonesty, cruelty, and neglect of conscience, nothing but praise can be given to that intention.'—*Morning Post.*
GOD'S GOOD MAN: A SIMPLE LOVE STORY. *Sixth Edition.*

Anthony Hope's Novels
Crown 8vo. 6s. each.

THE GOD IN THE CAR. *Tenth Edition.*
'A very remarkable book, deserving of critical analysis impossible within our limit; brilliant, but not superficial; well considered, but not elaborated; constructed with the proverbial art that conceals, but yet allows itself to be enjoyed by readers to whom fine literary method is a keen pleasure.'—*The World.*
A CHANGE OF AIR. *Sixth Edition.*
'A graceful, vivacious comedy, true to human nature. The characters are traced with a masterly hand.'—*Times.*
A MAN OF MARK. *Fifth Edition.*
'Of all Mr. Hope's books, "A Man of Mark" is the one which best compares with The Prisoner of Zenda."'—*National Observer.*

THE CHRONICLES OF COUNT ANTONIO. *Fifth Edition.*
'It is a perfectly enchanting story of love and chivalry, and pure romance. The Count is the most constant, desperate, and modest and tender of lovers, a peerless gentleman, an intrepid fighter, a faithful friend, and a magnanimous foe.'—*Guardian.*

PHROSO. Illustrated by H. R. MILLAR. *Sixth Edition.*
'The tale is thoroughly fresh, quick with vitality, stirring the blood.'—*St. James's Gazette.*

SIMON DALE. Illustrated. *Sixth Edition.*
'There is searching analysis of human nature, with a most ingeniously constructed plot. Mr. Hope has drawn the contrasts of his women with marvellous subtlety and delicacy.' —*Times.*

THE KING'S MIRROR. *Fourth Edition.*
'In elegance, delicacy, and tact it ranks with the best of his novels, while in the wide range of its portraiture and the subtilty of its analysis it surpasses all his earlier ventures.' —*Spectator.*

QUISANTE. *Fourth Edition.*
'The book is notable for a very high literary quality, and an impress of power and mastery on every page.'—*Daily Chronicle.*

THE DOLLY DIALOGUES.

W. W. Jacobs' Novels
Crown 8vo. 3s. 6d. each.

MANY CARGOES. *Twenty-Seventh Edition.*
SEA URCHINS. *Eleventh Edition.*
A MASTER OF CRAFT. Illustrated. *Sixth Edition.*
'Can be unreservedly recommended to all who have not lost their appetite for wholesome laughter.'—*Spectator.*
'The best humorous book published for many a day.'—*Black and White.*

LIGHT FREIGHTS. Illustrated. *Fourth Edition.*
'His wit and humour are perfectly irresistible. Mr. Jacobs writes of skippers, and mates, and seamen, and his crew are the jolliest lot that ever sailed.'—*Daily News.*
'Laughter in every page.'—*Daily Mail.*

Lucas Malet's Novels
Crown 8vo. 6s. each.

COLONEL ENDERBY'S WIFE. *Third Edition.*
A COUNSEL OF PERFECTION. *New Edition.*
LITTLE PETER. *Second Edition.* 3s. 6d.
THE WAGES OF SIN. *Fourteenth Edition.*
THE CARISSIMA. *Fourth Edition.*
THE GATELESS BARRIER. *Fourth Edition.*
'In "The Gateless Barrier" it is at once evident that, whilst Lucas Malet has preserved her birthright of originality, the artistry, the actual writing, is above even the high level of the books that were born before.'—*Westminster Gazette.*

THE HISTORY OF SIR RICHARD CALMADY. *Seventh Edition.* A Limited Edition in Two Volumes. *Crown 8vo.* 12s.
'A picture finely and amply conceived. In the strength and insight in which the story has been conceived, in the wealth of fancy and reflection bestowed upon its execution, and in the moving sincerity of its pathos throughout, "Sir Richard Calmady" must rank as the great novel of a great writer.'—*Literature.*
'The ripest fruit of Lucas Malet's genius. A picture of maternal love by turns tender and terrible.'—*Spectator.*
'A remarkably fine book, with a noble motive and a sound conclusion.'—*Pilot.*

Gilbert Parker's Novels
Crown 8vo. 6s. each.

PIERRE AND HIS PEOPLE. *Fifth Edition.*
'Stories happily conceived and finely executed. There is strength and genius in Mr Parker's style.'—*Daily Telegraph.*

MRS. FALCHION. *Fifth Edition.*
'A splendid study of character.'—*Athenæum.*

THE TRANSLATION OF A SAVAGE. *Second Edition.*
THE TRAIL OF THE SWORD. Illustrated. *Eighth Edition.*
'A rousing and dramatic tale. A book like this is a joy inexpressible.'—*Daily Chronicle.*

WHEN VALMOND CAME TO PONTIAC: The Story of a Lost Napoleon. *Fifth Edition.*
'Here we find romance—real, breathing, living romance. The character of Valmond is drawn unerringly.'—*Pall Mall Gazette.*
AN ADVENTURER OF THE NORTH: The Last Adventures of 'Pretty Pierre.' *Third Edition.*
'The present book is full of fine and moving stories of the great North.'—*Glasgow Herald.*
THE SEATS OF THE MIGHTY. Illustrated. *Thirteenth Edition.*
'Mr. Parker has produced a really fine historical novel.'—*Athenæum.*
'A great book.'—*Black and White.*
THE BATTLE OF THE STRONG: a Romance of Two Kingdoms. Illustrated. *Fourth Edition.*
'Nothing more vigorous or more human has come from Mr. Gilbert Parker than this novel.'—*Literature.*
THE POMP OF THE LAVILETTES. *Second Edition.* 3s. 6d.
'Unforced pathos, and a deeper knowledge of human nature than he has displayed before.'
—*Pall Mall Gazette.*

Arthur Morrison's Novels
Crown 8vo. 6s. each.

TALES OF MEAN STREETS. *Sixth Edition.*
'A great book. The author's method is amazingly effective, and produces a thrilling sense of reality. The writer lays upon us a master hand. The book is simply appalling and irresistible in its interest. It is humorous also; without humour it would not make the mark it is certain to make.'—*World.*
A CHILD OF THE JAGO. *Fourth Edition.*
'The book is a masterpiece.'—*Pall Mall Gazette.*
TO LONDON TOWN. *Second Edition.*
'This is the new Mr. Arthur Morrison, gracious and tender, sympathetic and human.'—
Daily Telegraph.
CUNNING MURRELL.
'Admirable. . . Delightful humorous relief . . . a most artistic and satisfactory achievement.'—*Spectator.*
THE HOLE IN THE WALL. *Third Edition.*
'A masterpiece of artistic realism. It has a finality of touch that only a master may command.'—*Daily Chronicle.*
'An absolute masterpiece, which any novelist might be proud to claim.'—*Graphic.*
'"The Hole in the Wall" is a masterly piece of work. His characters are drawn with amazing skill. Extraordinary power.'—*Daily Telegraph.*

Eden Phillpotts' Novels
Crown 8vo. 6s. each.

LYING PROPHETS.
CHILDREN OF THE MIST. *Fifth Edition.*
THE HUMAN BOY. With a Frontispiece. *Fourth Edition.*
'Mr. Phillpotts knows exactly what school-boys do, and can lay bare their inmost thoughts; likewise he shows an all-pervading sense of humour.'—*Academy.*
SONS OF THE MORNING. *Second Edition.*
'A book of strange power and fascination.'—*Morning Post.*
THE STRIKING HOURS. *Second Edition.*
'Tragedy and comedy, pathos and humour, are blended to a nicety in this volume.'—*World.*
'The whole book is redolent of a fresher and ampler air than breathes in the circumscribed life of great towns.'—*Spectator.*
THE RIVER. *Third Edition.*
'"The River" places Mr. Phillpotts in the front rank of living novelists.'—*Punch.*
'Since "Lorna Doone" we have had nothing so picturesque as this new romance.'—*Birmingham Gazette.*
'Mr. Phillpotts's new book is a masterpiece which brings him indisputably into the front rank of English novelists.'—*Pall Mall Gazette.*
'This great romance of the River Dart. The finest book Mr. Eden Phillpotts has written.'
—*Morning Post.*
THE AMERICAN PRISONER. *Third Edition.*
THE SECRET WOMAN. *Second Edition.*

S. Baring-Gould's Novels
Crown 8vo.   6s. each.

ARMINELL. *Fifth Edition.*
URITH. *Fifth Edition.*
IN THE ROAR OF THE SEA. *Seventh Edition.*
CHEAP JACK ZITA. *Fourth Edition.*
MARGERY OF QUETHER. *Third Edition.*
THE QUEEN OF LOVE. *Fifth Edition.*
JACQUETTA. *Third Edition.*
KITTY ALONE. *Fifth Edition.*
NOÉMI. Illustrated. *Fourth Edition.*
THE BROOM-SQUIRE. Illustrated. *Fourth Edition.*
DARTMOOR IDYLLS.

THE PENNYCOMEQUICKS. *Third Edition.*
GUAVAS THE TINNER. Illustrated. *Second Edition.*
BLADYS. Illustrated. *Second Edition.*
DOMITIA. Illustrated. *Second Edition.*
PABO THE PRIEST.
WINIFRED. Illustrated. *Second Edition.*
THE FROBISHERS.
ROYAL GEORGIE. Illustrated.
MISS QUILLET. Illustrated.
LITTLE TU'PENNY. *A New Edition.* 6d.
CHRIS OF ALL SORTS.
IN DEWISLAND. *Second Edition.*

Robert Barr's Novels
Crown 8vo.   6s. each.

IN THE MIDST OF ALARMS. *Third Edition.*
  'A book which has abundantly satisfied us by its capital humour.'—*Daily Chronicle.*
THE MUTABLE MANY. *Second Edition.*
  'There is much insight in it, and much excellent humour.'—*Daily Chronicle.*
THE VICTORS.
THE COUNTESS TEKLA. *Third Edition.*
  'Of these mediæval romances, which are now gaining ground, "The Countess Tekla"
is the very best we have seen.'—*Pall Mall Gazette.*
THE LADY ELECTRA. *Second Edition.*
THE TEMPESTUOUS PETTICOAT.

E. Maria Albanesi's Novels
Crown 8vo.   6s. each.

SUSANNAH AND ONE OTHER. *Fourth Edition.*
THE BLUNDER OF AN INNOCENT. *Second Edition.*
CAPRICIOUS CAROLINE. *Second Edition.*
LOVE AND LOUISA. *Second Edition.*
PETER, A PARASITE.

B. M. Croker's Novels
Crown 8vo.   6s. each.

ANGEL. *Fourth Edition.*
PEGGY OF THE BARTONS. *Sixth Edit.*
THE OLD CANTONMENT.

A STATE SECRET. *Third Edition.*
JOHANNA. *Second Edition.*
THE HAPPY VALLEY. *Second Edition.*

J. H. Findlater's Novels
Crown 8vo.   6s. each.

THE GREEN GRAVES OF BALGOWRIE. *Fifth Edition.*

Mary Findlater's Novels
Crown 8vo.   6s.

A NARROW WAY. *Third Edition.*
OVER THE HILLS.

THE ROSE OF JOY. *Second Edition.*

Robert Hichens' Novels
Crown 8vo.   6s. each.

THE PROPHET OF BERKELEY SQUARE. *Second Edition*
TONGUES OF CONSCIENCE. *Second Edition.*
FELIX. *Fourth Edition.*
THE WOMAN WITH THE FAN. *Fifth Edition.*
BYEWAYS. 3s. 6d.
THE GARDEN OF ALLAH *Seventh Edition.*

Henry James's Novels
Crown 8vo. 6s. each.

THE SOFT SIDE. *Second Edition.*
THE BETTER SORT.

THE AMBASSADORS. *Second Edition.*
THE GOLDEN BOWL.

Mary E. Mann's Novels
Crown 8vo. 6s. each.

OLIVIA'S SUMMER. *Second Edition.*
A LOST ESTATE. *A New Edition.*
THE PARISH OF HILBY. *A New Edition.*
*THE PARISH NURSE.
GRAN'MA'S JANE.
MRS. PETER HOWARD.

A WINTER'S TALE. *A New Edition.*
ONE ANOTHER'S BURDENS. *A New Edition.*
THERE WAS ONCE A PRINCE. Illustrated. 3s 6d.
WHEN ARNOLD COMES HOME. Illustrated. 3s. 6d.

W. Pett Ridge's Novels
Crown 8vo. 6s. each.

LOST PROPERTY. *Second Edition.*
ERB. *Second Edition.*
A SON OF THE STATE. 3s. 6d.

A BREAKER OF LAWS. 3s. 6d.
MRS. GALER'S BUSINESS.
SECRETARY TO BAYNE, M.P. 3s. 6d.

Adeline Sergeant's Novels
Crown 8vo. 6s. each.

THE MASTER OF BEECHWOOD.
BARBARA'S MONEY. *Second Edition.*
ANTHEA'S WAY.
THE YELLOW DIAMOND. *Second Edition.*
UNDER SUSPICION.

THE LOVE THAT OVERCAME.
THE ENTHUSIAST.
ACCUSED AND ACCUSER. *Second Edition.*
THE PROGRESS OF RACHEL.
THE MYSTERY OF THE MOAT.

THE MYSTERY OF A BUNGALOW. *Second Edition. Crown 8vo. 6s.*
Clifford (Hugh). A FREE LANCE OF TO-DAY. *Crown 8vo. 6s.*
Clifford (Mrs. W. K.). See also Shilling Novels and Books for Boys and Girls.
Cobb (Thomas). A CHANGE OF FACE. *Crown 8vo. 6s.*
Cobban (J. Maclaren). See Shilling Novels.
Corelli (Marie). See page 32.
Cotes (Mrs. Everard). See Sara Jeannette Duncan.
Cotterell (Constance). THE VIRGIN AND THE SCALES. *Crown 8vo. 6s.*
Crane (Stephen) and Barr (Robert). THE O'RUDDY. *Crown 8vo. 6s.*
Crockett (S. R.), Author of 'The Raiders,' etc. LOCHINVAR. Illustrated. *Second Edition. Crown 8vo. 6s.*
THE STANDARD BEARER. *Crown 8vo. 6s.*
Croker (B. M.). See page 35.
Dawson (A. J.). DANIEL WHYTE. *Crown 8vo. 3s. 6d.*
Doyle (A. Conan), Author of 'Sherlock Holmes,' 'The White Company,' etc. ROUND THE RED LAMP. *Ninth Edition. Crown 8vo. 6s.*
Duncan (Sara Jeannette) (Mrs. Everard Cotes). THOSE DELIGHTFUL AMERI-CANS. Illustrated. *Third Edition. Crown 8vo. 6s.*
THE POOL IN THE DESERT. *Crown 8vo. 6s.*
A VOYAGE OF CONSOLATION. *Crown 8vo. 3s. 6d.*
Findlater (J. H.). See page 35 and Shilling Novels.
Findlater (Mary). See page 35.
Fitzpatrick (K.) THE WEANS AT ROWALLAN. Illustrated. *Crown 8vo. 6s.*
Fitzstephen (Gerald). MORE KIN THAN KIND. *Crown 8vo. 6s.*
Fletcher (J. S.). LUCIAN THE DREAMER. *Crown 8vo. 6s.*
DAVID MARCH. *Crown 8vo. 6s.*
Francis (M. E.). See Shilling Novels.
Fraser (Mrs. Hugh), Author of 'The Stolen Emperor.' THE SLAKING OF THE SWORD. *Crown 8vo. 6s.*
Gallon (Tom), Author of 'Kiddy.' RICKERBY'S FOLLY. *Crown 8vo. 6s.*
Gerard (Dorothea), Author of 'Lady Baby.' THE CONQUEST OF LONDON. *Second Edition. Crown 8vo. 6s.*
HOLY MATRIMONY. *Second Edition. Crown 8vo. 6s.*
MADE OF MONEY. *Crown 8vo. 6s.*

Gerard (Emily). THE HERONS' TOWER. *Crown 8vo. 6s.*
Gissing (George), Author of 'Demos,' 'In the Year of Jubilee,' etc. THE TOWN TRAVELLER. *Second Edition. Crown 8vo. 6s.*
THE CROWN OF LIFE. *Crown 8vo. 6s.*
Glanville (Ernest). THE INCA'S TREASURE. Illustrated. *Crown 8vo. 3s. 6d.*
Gleig (Charles). BUNTER'S CRUISE. Illustrated. *Crown 8vo. 3s. 6d.*
Goss (C. F.). See Shilling Novels.
Herbertson (Agnes G.). PATIENCE DEAN. *Crown 8vo. 6s.*
Hichens (Robert). See page 35.
Hobbes (John Oliver), Author of 'Robert Orange.' THE SERIOUS WOOING. *Crown 8vo. 6s.*
Hope (Anthony). See page 32.
Hough (Emerson). THE MISSISSIPPI BUBBLE. Illustrated. *Crown 8vo. 6s.*
Hyne (C. J. Cutcliffe), Author of 'Captain Kettle.' MR. HORROCKS, PURSER. *Third Edition. Crown 8vo. 6s.*
Jacobs (W. W.). See page 33.
James (Henry). See page 36.
Janson (Gustaf). ABRAHAM'S SACRIFICE. *Crown 8vo. 6s.*
Keays (H. A. Mitchell). HE THAT EATETH BREAD WITH ME. *Crown 8vo. 6s.*
Lawless (Hon. Emily). See Shilling Novels.
Lawson (Harry), Author of 'When the Billy Boils.' CHILDREN OF THE BUSH. *Crown 8vo. 6s.*
Levett-Yeats (S.). ORRAIN. *Second Edition. Crown 8vo. 6s.*
Linden (Annie). A WOMAN OF SENTIMENT. *Crown 8vo. 6s.*
Linton (E. Lynn). THE TRUE HISTORY OF JOSHUA DAVIDSON, Christian and Communist. *Twelfth Edition. Medium 8vo. 6d.*
Long (J. Luther), Co-Author of 'The Darling of the Gods.' MADAME BUTTERFLY. *Crown 8vo. 3s. 6d.*
SIXTY JANE. *Crown 8vo. 6s.*
Lyall (Edna). DERRICK VAUGHAN, NOVELIST. *42nd Thousand. Cr. 8vo. 3s. 6d.*

M'Carthy (Justin H.), Author of ' If I were King.' THE LADY OF LOYALTY HOUSE. *Third Edition. Crown 8vo. 6s.*
THE DRYAD. *Crown 8vo. 6s.*
Mackie (Pauline Bradford). THE VOICE IN THE DESERT. *Crown 8vo. 6s.*
Macnaughtan (S.). THE FORTUNE OF CHRISTINA MACNAB. *Third Edition. Crown 8vo. 6s.*
Malet (Lucas). See page 33.
Mann (Mrs. M. E.). See page 36.
Marriott (Charles), Author of 'The Column. GENEVRA. *Second Edition. Cr. 8vo. 6s.*
Marsh (Richard). THE TWICKENHAM PEERAGE. *Second Edition. Crown 8vo. 6s.*
A METAMORPHOSIS. *Crown 8vo. 6s.*
GARNERED. *Crown 8vo. 6s.*
A DUEL. *Crown 8vo. 6s.*
Mason (A. E. W.), Author of 'The Courtship of Morrice Buckler,' 'Miranda of the Balcony, etc. CLEMENTINA. Illustrated. *Crown 8vo. Second Edition. 6s.*
Mathers (Helen), Author of 'Comin' thro' the Rye.' HONEY. *Fourth Edition. Crown 8vo. 6s.*
GRIFF OF GRIFFITHSCOURT. *Crown 8vo. 6s.*
Meade (L. T.). DRIFT. *Crown 8vo. 6s.*
RESURGAM. *Crown 8vo. 6s.*
Meredith (Ellis). HEART OF MY HEART. *Crown 8vo. 6s.*
'Miss Molly' (The Author of). THE GREAT RECONCILER. *Crown 8vo. 6s.*
Mitford (Bertram). THE SIGN OF THE SPIDER. Illustrated. *Sixth Edition Crown 8vo. 3s. 6d.*
IN THE WHIRL OF THE RISING. *Third Edition. Crown 8vo. 6s.*
THE RED DERELICT. *Crown 8vo. 6s.*
Montresor (F. F.), Author of 'Into the Highways and Hedges.' THE ALIEN. *Third Edition. Crown 8vo. 6s.*
Morrison (Arthur). See page 34.
Nesbit (E.). (Mrs. E. Bland). THE RED HOUSE. Illustrated. *Fourth Edition. Crown 8vo. 6s.*
THE LITERARY SENSE. *Crown 8vo. 6s.*
Norris (W. E.). THE CREDIT OF THE COUNTY. Illustrated. *Second Edition. Crown 8vo. 6s.*
THE EMBARRASSING ORPHAN. *Crown 8vo. 6s.*
NIGEL'S VOCATION. *Crown 8vo. 6s.*
LORD LEONARD THE LUCKLESS. *Crown 8vo. 6s.*
BARHAM OF BELTANA. *Crown 8vo. 6s.*
Oliphant (Mrs.). See Shilling Novels.
Ollivant (Alfred). OWD BOB, THE GREY DOG OF KENMUIR. *Seventh Edition. Crown 8vo. 6s.*
Oppenheim (E. Phillips). MASTER OF MEN. *Third Edition. Crown 8vo. 6s.*
Oxenham (John), Author of 'Barbe of Grand Bayou.' A WEAVER OF WEBS. *Second Edition. Crown 8vo. 6s.*
THE GATE OF THE DESERT. *Crown 8vo. 6s.*
Pain (Barry). THREE FANTASIES. *Crown 8vo. 1s.*
LINDLEY KAYS. *Third Edition. Crown 8vo. 6s.*
Parker (Gilbert). See page 23.
Pemberton (Max). THE FOOTSTEPS OF A THRONE. Illustrated. *Third Edition. Crown 8vo. 6s.*
I CROWN THEE KING. With Illustrations by Frank Dadd and A. Forrestier. *Crown 8vo. 6s.*
Penny (Mrs. F. E.). See Shilling Novels.
Phillpotts (Eden). See page 34, and Shilling Novels.
Pickthall (Marmaduke). SAID THE FISHERMAN. *Fifth Edition. Crown 8vo. 6s.*
*BRENDLE. *Crown 8vo. 6s.*
*Pryce (Richard). WINIFRED MOUNT. *A New Edition. Crown 8vo. 6s.*
'Q,' Author of 'Dead Man's Rock.' THE WHITE WOLF. *Second Edition. Crown 8vo. 6s.*
Queux (W. le). THE HUNCHBACK OF WESTMINSTER. *Third Edition. Crown 8vo. 6s.*
THE CLOSED BOOK. *Second Edition. Crown 8vo. 6s.*
THE VALLEY OF THE SHADOW. Illustrated. *Crown 8vo. 6s.*
Rhys (Grace). THE WOOING OF SHEILA. *Second Edition. Crown 8vo. 6s.*
THE PRINCE OF LISNOVER. *Crown 8vo. 6s.*